CASE STUDIES IN

CULTURAL ANTHROPOLOGY

GENERAL EDITORS
George and Louise Spindler
STANFORD UNIVERSITY

A VILLAGE IN MALTA

CENTRAL MEDITERRANEAN

CORSICA

SARDINIA

ITALY

SICILY

TUNISIA

GOZO ○ MALTA

GREECE

FERRY

St. Paul's Bay

FERRY

COMINO

GOZO

Żebbuġ
Gharb
Ghasri
San Lawrenz
Kercem
Munxar
Sannat
Rabat
Xewkija
Xagħra
Nadur
Qala
Ghajnsielem

Mellieħa
Mġarr
Naxxar
Mosta
Mdina
Rabat
Dingli
Attard
Balzan
Lija
Għargħur
Birkirkara
Qormi
Siġġiewi
Żebbuġ
Qrendi

St. Julian's
Sliema
Gżira
Msida
Santa Venera
Ħamrun
Paola
Marsa
Luqa
Kirkop
Mqabba
Safi
Żurrieq

Valletta
Floriana
Pietà
Senglea
Cospicua
Vittoriosa
Kalkara
Żabbar
Tarxien
Gudja
Ghaxaq
Żejtun
Marsaskala
Marsaxlokk
Birżebbuġa

MALTA

LEGEND
—— Main roads
– – – Secondary roads
· · · · · Parish boundaries
▒ Built-up areas

0 1 2 3 4 5 MILES

MALTA AND GOZO

A Village in Malta

FIELDWORK EDITION

By

JEREMY BOISSEVAIN
University of Amsterdam

HOLT, RINEHART AND WINSTON

NEW YORK   CHICAGO   SAN FRANCISCO   DALLAS
MONTREAL   TORONTO   LONDON   SYDNEY

Cover photograph: *Standard-bearer and members of the Confraternity of the Blessed Sacrament during the Translation of the relic on the eve of the feast of Saint Martin.*

Library of Congress Cataloging in Publication Data

Boissevain, Jeremy.
   A village in Malta.

   (Case studies in cultural anthropology)
   First published in 1969 under title: Hal-Farrug.
   The author's "Fieldwork in Malta," (chapter 9) was
previously published in 1970 in Being an anthropologist,
edited by G. D. Spindler.
   Bibliography: p. 133
   1.   Malta—Social life and customs.   I.   Title.
II.   Series.
DG994.B68   1980   945.8'5   79-21054
ISBN 0-03-053411-9

To the memory of my father
Cornelis Alfred Boissevain

Foreword

About the Series

These case studies in cultural anthropology are designed to bring to students, in beginning and intermediate courses in the social sciences, insights into the richness and complexity of human life as it is lived in different ways and in different places. They are written by men and women who have lived in the societies they write about and who are professionally trained as observers and interpreters of human behavior. The authors are also teachers, and in writing their books they have kept the students who will read them foremost in their minds. It is our belief that when an understanding of ways of life very different from one's own is gained, abstractions and generalizations about social structure, cultural values, subsistence techniques, and the other universal categories of human social behavior become meaningful.

About the Author

London-born Jeremy Boissevain is Professor of Social Anthropology at the University of Amsterdam, Holland, having previously taught at the Université de Montréal in Canada and the new University of Sussex in England. After graduating in 1952 from Haverford College, where he studied romance languages, he served for almost six years as CARE mission chief in the Philippines, Japan, India, and finally Malta. He resigned in 1958 to begin graduate work in social anthropology at the London School of Economics and Political Science. He obtained his Ph.D. in 1962 for his study of local politics in Malta. In addition, he has carried out field research in the Fezzan desert in Libya, in an isolated agrotown in Sicily, and among Italian-Canadians in Montreal. He has recently published a book about what he calls the neglected "nongroups" in the social sciences: networks and coalitions, which is based partly upon his field research in Malta.* He is married and has four daughters, two of whom were born in Malta.

About the Book

A Village in Malta is timely. This small island society is becoming industrialized, as are so many small communities elsewhere in the world today. Malta is unique, however, in the Mediterranean context, in that there is a high literacy rate and an economy that has for many centuries been based on the services its people provided to foreign garrisons rather than exclusively through agriculture. Until Malta achieved independence from Britain in 1964, the island was essentially a fortress in the hands

* *Friends of Friends: Networks, Manipulators and Coalitions*. Oxford: Basil Blackwell, 1974.

of the British naval forces, and before that, but for a brief interlude, had long been the seat of the famed Knights of Malta. It has been a bastion between the Christian and the Moslem worlds, and strongly influenced by the cultures of both. Although the language of Malta is Semitic, the main features of Maltese culture are southern European. This congeries of forces, historical and geographical in nature, make the processes of modernization special in Malta, and in Hal-Farrug, the focus of this case study.

Boissevain's approach is structural, as he analyzes the basic institutions of Hal-Farrug. His analysis is given vitality and meaning by the inclusion of extensive case materials collected from individuals and families, and about specific events. Individuals, he writes, ". . . provide the social cement which holds the groups and institutions of society together." The social facts are given life by the descriptions of real people in real situations: Carmel Abela courting his future wife; Victor Azzopardi collecting funds for St. Martin's feast day; Dun Gorg, the parish priest, involved in solving the problems of a committee composed of dissident factions.

Dr. Boissevain continues to complement the analyses at the institutional level with those at the individual level. For example, when dealing with changes taking place in the family, he not only relates these to changes taking place in other social sectors, such as the economic system, but analyzes the structural forms in terms of individual choices. In dealing with the area of family relations, he points out that the structural form is a reflection of pragmatic choices. He writes that these choices are made not only in answer to the question "What is expected of me by others in this particular situation?" but also to such questions as "What is best for me and my family?" "From what possibility will I derive the greatest benefit?" "How much can I get away with?" And these considerations illustrate the importance of the consideration of individual variability.

An important theme running throughout the case study is the importance of the Catholic Church—its role as played in the family, and in economic, social, and political areas. Most of the people of Farrug regulate their lives by the periodic religious activities. "There is a very tight fit between what should be and what is, between the teaching of the Church and the moral code of the people of Farrug."

The book contains an interesting analysis of political contests, using the terminology of game playing. Relationhips between national politics and parish politics are drawn as the author describes how "the encapsulated rural village" is being absorbed into the nation.

The last chapter makes a point of particular theoretical importance. Here, the author explains that the study has focused upon a village, but what has emerged is a realization of the importance of the individual. He concludes that the integration of communities and groups into the whole which we call "society" takes place via the personal networks of individuals which constitute the communities.

This case study is therefore a particularly significant addition to the series. It provides for the first time in the series an example of a Mediterranean culture where the Moslem and Christian traditions meet. It also makes a useful methodological contribution by showing how the anthropologist, by attention to both the behavior of the people he is observing and the answers to the questions he asks these people, even when behaviors and answers produce conflicting evidence, can generate predictive statements—that under certain conditions a given set of interdependent behaviors will tend to take place. The anthropologist is therefore, due to his objective perspective on the culture and the relatively great freedom of inquiry resident in his role, able to make generalizations about the behavior of the people he is studying, and their community, that they themselves are not able to make. The case study is also of particular importance methodologically because it demonstrates so clearly how abstractions and generalizations are made human and believable, as well as scientifically valid, by documentation at the particularistic, local, processual level. Specific people and real events document all generalizations in this study. Every reader will gain from this case study some insight into the meaning of the ethnographer's role as participant observer. Dr. Boissevain knows his community as a resident, as a friend of individuals and families, and as an on-the-spot observer of social, political, and religious events.

Fieldwork Edition

As Chapter 9 in this case study, we have added "Fieldwork in Malta," from *Being An Anthropologist: Fieldwork in Eleven Cultures,* edited by George Spindler. The authors contributing to this volume were asked to tell of their personal experiences in the field, of their relationships with the people they were studying, how they explained themselves and their research to the people, and of their place in the community. Jeremy Boissevain has answered these questions well. The reader will gain an understanding of how these aspects of ethnographic fieldwork may influence both the information which is collected and its interpretation. More often than not, however, the frank discussion of the exigencies of fieldwork that makes such understanding possible is missing from the finished ethnography which colleagues and students read. This enhanced case study puts the reader in direct contact with the reality of the ethnographer's experience.

As teachers of introductory cultural anthropology at Stanford University, we have often used the case studies and their related fieldwork chapters as instructional units, with good effect. We think they make a most useful combination, and now they are conveniently bound together within the same cover.

GEORGE AND LOUISE SPINDLER
General Editors

Calistoga, California

Preface

The initial research upon which this book is based was carried out in Malta between July 1960 and September 1961 under the terms of a grant from the British Colonial Science Research Council. The present study was first presented as a course of lectures to first- and second-year students at the University of Amsterdam during the 1967 spring term. Although I have occasionally drawn on material published in my earlier volume *Saints and Fireworks: Religion and Politics in Rural Malta* (1965), most of the material presented here, as well as its underlying framework, is new. The generosity of the Wenner-Gren Foundation for Anthropological Research made it possible for me to revisit Malta during the summer of 1967 and to make a short restudy of Hal-Farrug. Several of the sections were reworked and discussed with Maltese friends.

Malta is changing very rapidly. Most of the changes brought about by Malta's independence and the second Vatican council have not yet found their way into these pages. I shall deal with them later. Except where I mention it specifically, the present account is based upon the research I conducted in 1960. The social time is thus that of the early 1960s.

I owe a great deal to Francis Mizzi, whose hard work, companionship, and penetrating analysis of his own social environment have been invaluable. My family participated fully in the fieldwork and the various periods of working it out. I am especially grateful to my wife for helping me to correct the many drafts and providing me with the right word at the right time. To the Royal University of Malta, and in particular to Professor Salvino Busuttil I owe special thanks for providing me with research facilities during the summer of 1967. Without the splendid isolation of the little room known as the "yellow submarine" this book could not yet have appeared. Miss Trudy van der Sluis kindly transcribed the first draft and typed the manuscript. Rudo Niemeyer provided technical assistance on statistical matters and H. M. van Groos drew the map and diagram. I have also benefited greatly from the criticism of Joseph Cassar Pullicino, Peter Serracino-Inglott, Albert Trouwborst, and Charles Vella, all of whom read and commented on the manuscript. The interpretation and any shortcomings are, of course, my own responsibility.

Finally, I would like once again to thank the people of Hal-Farrug, who welcomed us in 1960 and again in 1967. We will always be grateful for the friendliness and help they gave us on both occasions. To protect their privacy I have changed all names, including that of the village (although a Hal-Farrug actually existed nearby some centuries ago). I hope the readers will respect their privacy as well. I offer this book in the hope that it will help further greater understanding between the Maltese themselves and between the Maltese and those beyond their shores.

Amsterdam, Holland   Jeremy Boissevain
December 1968

Contents

CASE STUDIES IN

CULTURAL ANTHROPOLOGY

GENERAL EDITORS
George and Louise Spindler
STANFORD UNIVERSITY

A VILLAGE IN MALTA

Introduction

THIS IS A STUDY of a village in a small island society situated in the center of the Mediterranean. The Mediterranean has only recently begun to attract the attention of anthropologists. This new focus is partly the result of a wish to learn more about the cultures and social institutions which have left such an imprint on North, South, and Middle America. It is also partly the result of the contact that experienced Anglo-American anthropologists, and persons who were to become anthropologists, had with this area during the war. Perhaps most important of all, however, it is a reflection of the growing maturity of a relatively young discipline. Anthropologists are coming to realize that anthropology is the study of all mankind, not just of primitive, peasant, or non-Western man.

Malta's high degree of literacy, its many specialized occupations, its bilateral kinship system, its wealth of voluntary associations, provide a fascinating contrast to the primitive societies studied so often by anthropologists. This book thus furnishes comparative case material on such institutions as the family, social differentiation, religion, associations, and political structure. It is also of interest to those particuarly concerned with the Mediterranean region. It describes a society well along the road to industrialization. In this Malta differs from many of the countries around it. Most of the people bordering on the Mediterranean (studied by anthropologists) derive their livelihood from agriculture. Malta's economy, in contrast, has for many centuries been based on the services its people provided to foreign garrisons.

One of the book's themes is the way in which Malta's increasing tempo of industrialization is affecting its social institutions. Another theme is the important role that the choices and actions of *individuals*—as contrasted to *groups* (upon which anthropological analysis normally focuses)—play in generating social forms and patterns of behavior. The social position of the church in this most Catholic society provides a third important theme. The position of the Church in Malta today is in many respects similar to the role it occupied once in Europe, when all countries

1

were Catholic. It is another way in which Malta may be contrasted with surrounding societies, where secularization is much further advanced.

It is important to keep in mind that this is a study of a village, for one-half of Malta's population lives in the great urban agglomeration surrounding Valletta and the Grand Harbour. There is still a marked difference in values, dress, and even speech between those who live in this area and those who live in the villages. It is legitimate to ask how far the description and generalizations advanced about one village hold true for other villages, and for all of Malta. This is a problem which most fieldworkers face. I attempted to resolve it by living in a second village for an equal length of time. I also made short comparative studies in ten other villages and two urban areas, but it is important to remember that this book deals only with a part of Malta. The way of life which it describes is unfamiliar, if not unknown, to the urban Maltese middle and upper classes. They are separated from the villagers in both geographical and social terms.

The case study begins with a brief treatment of Malta in time and space. It then examines the way in which Maltese in general and the people of Farrug in particular earn their living. It moves on to look at the family, the wider network of relations, and the way in which new kinsmen are acquired through marriage, which is viewed as a game of strategy. The social distinctions that the apparently egalitarian people of Farrug use to set themselves apart from each other are also examined. The focus then shifts to the role of religion and church in the village. After examining the religious and secular groups and institutions which give a certain structural form to the village, the conflict between the partisans of rival saints, band clubs, and political factions in the village is discussed. A final chapter deals with the way Farrug is connected with and forms part of the nation as a whole and the important part individuals play in this process. It also compares Farrug to its neighbors, for it is both similar and unique.

1

The Background

Malta

LAND AND PEOPLE. The Maltese islands—consisting of Malta, Gozo, Comino, Cominotto, and Filfla—lie midway between Gibraltar and Lebanon, at almost the exact geographical center of the Mediterranean. Sicily lies just 58 miles to the north, Tripoli 220 miles due south, and Tunis slightly over 200 miles to the west. The islands thus form a port of call between Europe and North Africa, a strategic and cultural bastion between the Christian and Moslem worlds. The Maltese have been in touch with both for centuries, and the cultures of both have contributed many traits and characteristics which the islanders have adapted to their own use.

The language, for example, is Semitic and closely related to North African Arabic. This undoubtedly reflects Malta's close contact in the past with its southern neighbors. Yet the main features of the culture and the social organization of the people who speak this language place them squarely within the Latin or southern European portion of the Mediterranean region.

Malta, the largest and southernmost island, is 17 miles long and 9 miles wide, and covers an area of 95 square miles. Gozo is only 9 miles long, 5 miles wide, with an area of 26 square miles. The little islands of Comino and Cominotto, which lie in the 3-mile-wide channel separating the two main islands, have an area together of 1 square mile. Finally, Filfla, a large uninhabited rock now used as target for gunnery practice, lies 3 miles off the southwest coast of Malta.

The islands are composed entirely of limestone, covered in most places by a thin layer of fertile soil. Although the land rises to just over 800 feet by the cliffs of Dingli, on the eastern shore, the terrain of the island itself is varied and often broken with jagged cliffs falling into narrow valleys which run out to level fields. There are no rivers or lakes. A visitor to the islands, especially during the long, dry Mediterranean summer, is struck by the apparent absence of vegetation and the rocky aspect of the countryside. This is in part a false impression, for although there are few trees, neat rubble retaining and boundary walls hide a network of small, intensively cultivated fields.

In 1960, just under 329,000 people lived on the islands' 122 square miles. By 1967, heavy emigration and a declining birth rate had reduced the population to 314,000. In spite of this relative decrease, the Maltese archipelago, with a population density of just under 2600 per square mile, is still one of the most thickly populated countries in the world. Slightly over half the population live in the urban area which centers on Valletta and the Grand Harbour. The rest, and the part to which the inhabitants of Farrug belong, live in clearly separated villages and towns outside the conurbation. The population of Gozo and Comino is 26,000.

The densely populated built-up area centers on Valletta, but many of the "villages" which lie outside this area are in reality rural towns with populations of up to 15,000, as in the case of Qormi. The Maltese do not distinguish linguistically between small villages and country towns; both are called "villages" (*rhula;* singular, *rahal,* or *Hal* for short, as in Hal-Farrug). These are contrasted with *Il-Belt,* the city of Valletta and its environs. Although town and country are contrasted, it is worthwhile pointing once again to Malta's small size. No village is more than an hour's bus ride from Valletta, and Gozo is only 30 minutes by ferry from its larger sister island. Moreover "rival" villages are often no more than a few hundred yards apart.

HISTORY. Malta's documented history stretches back over a thousand years. Throughout history the islands have been subject to many different rulers who sought to control their strategic position and fine natural harbors. Phoenicians, Carthaginians, Greeks, and Romans successively occupied the islands. In A.D. 870 the Arabs conquered the islands. Two hundred years later they were replaced by the Normans under Count Roger. After the death of the last Norman king, Malta shared the fate of Sicily and passed successively to the Swabians (1194–1266), the Angevins (1266–1283), the Aragonese (1283–1410), and the Castilians. In 1530, Emperor Charles V handed over Malta and Gozo with their protesting inhabitants as a fief in perpetuity to the Sovereign Military Order of St. John of Jerusalem, a powerful body of celibate nobles vowed to helping the poor, caring for the sick, and waging war on land and sea against Islam. Napoleon drove out the Knights in 1798, and in 1800 the British replaced the French. The islands were formally ceded to Britain under the terms of the Treaty of Paris in 1814. Finally, in 1964, the Maltese achieved their independence from Britain and for the first time entered the community of nations as an independent state.

Up until its independence, Malta was essentially a fortress in the hands of the strongest naval power in the Mediterranean. Its strategic position has to a very large extent influenced the economy and the political and administrative structure of the islands. A fortress requires a highly centralized administration, and this is what the Knights and Britain gave it.

Today, while there is a parliament composed of fifty elected regional representatives, there are still no municipal councils, headmen, or mayors to represent the interests of their respective villages and towns to higher authorities, or the wishes of these authorities to their fellow villagers and townsmen. Gozo provides a partial exception to this, for in 1961 an elected civic council was established. Because the council has no real power and is responsible for very little, however, it has not developed into an effective instrument of local government. In Malta, with the exception of the Post Office, Labour and Social Welfare, and Medical and Health departments, which maintain district offices in some of the larger centers, all government services are run from Valletta. Formal channels of contact between the administrative departments of the government in Valletta and the villages usually run via the Police Department, which maintains stations in all of Malta's towns, villages, and major hamlets. The district and local committees of the political parties, especially the government party, provide important informal communication channels. If, however, there are no elected or appointed spokesmen for individual villages and towns in the secular domain, there most certainly are in the religious domain. Parish priests have for centuries been the leading local figures.

Christianity was brought to Malta in A.D. 60 by Saint Paul, who was shipwrecked on Malta's northeast shore. The Maltese are intensely proud of the apostolic origin of their church. Except, possibly, for the 200-year period of Arab rule they have always been most devout Christians. The power and authority of the Church was greatly reinforced by the arrival of the Knights of St. John in 1530. Malta may be characterized as a theocracy during the period of the Knights, for the control of physical force, finance, justice, and the administrative departments of government were firmly in the hands of the Church or its representatives.

The relations between Britain and the Church in Malta were, on the whole, extremely cordial. Soon after her arrival, Britain imposed a mortmain law which forced the Church to sell off bequests of immovable property within one year of acquisition. It also abolished the right of sanctuary and restricted the jurisdiction of the ecclesiastical courts to purely spiritual matters, but the steps taken to restrict the great power of the Church were motivated by political pragmatism rather than the revolutionary ideals which had driven French administrators a few decades before to try to destroy the influence of the Church.

Britain, in fact, gave considerable protection to the Church in Malta. To begin with, it protected it from the competition of other religions. Protestant missionary activities were always severely restricted. Catholic precepts regarding education and marriage were also safeguarded: Education was based on Catholic religious principles and divorce and civil marriage were not permitted. The archbishop was accorded high honor, and in the jealously guarded order of precedence he was second only to the governor. Both the archbishop of Malta and the bishop of Gozo were exempted from the jurisdiction of the criminal courts. In spite of this protection, however, or perhaps because of it, anticlerical outbursts occurred during the only two relatively prolonged periods of self-government (1921–1930 and 1947–1958) permitted during the 150 years of British colonial rule.

The protection given to the Church by the Knights of Malta and Britain has been, on the whole, continued by the Nationalist government of independent Malta, elected in 1962 and again in 1966 with the support of the Church. The Church's interests in education, marriage, divorce, property, and maintaining Roman Catholicism as the official religion of the people of Malta, have been safeguarded.

Malta's economic development has been determined largely by its role as a fortress. It has a fortress economy. That is, it has been called upon to provide men to serve in and work for the island's garrison, whether Knights or British. It has also been called on to provide a large number of administrative personnel. Moreover, both Knights and British garrison had access to sources of funds outside of Malta. These made them largely independent of the rather precarious local economy. Malta has never been completely self-sufficient in food: It has always had to import grain, for example, to make bread, the basis of the local diet. For these various reasons we find that during the nineteenth century only about one in five of the economically active male population of Malta worked in agriculture, though the proportion rose as high as eight out of ten in many of the rural districts in both Gozo and Malta. During the first half of the last century cotton was king in Malta. Vineyards and olive groves were ripped out to plant cotton. The height of the Maltese cotton production came just before and during the American civil war when American cotton disappeared from the world market. The Maltese cotton industry was destroyed during the second half of the nineteenth century by the development of alternative cotton production centers in India and Egypt and the embargo placed upon Maltese goods, following several outbreaks of cholera in the islands. Although this was a period of hardship, the growing British military and naval garrison, the establishment of a large naval dockyard, and the development of Malta as an important bunkering station following the opening of the Suez canal provided an expanding field of economic activity.

At the turn of the century Malta, in contrast to its neighbors, was thus a semi-industrialized society. Today only one out of every ten persons is engaged in agriculture on a full-time basis, though there are still a few villages in Gozo and one in Malta (Mgarr) where more than half the population are full-time farmers.

Considering the peculiarities of Malta's centralized fortress administration and economy, it is not surprising that there has always existed a dichotomy between town and village. This was very marked during the rule of the Knights and British, for the city of Valletta—Il-Belt—and its environs formed the locus of ecclesiastical, economic, political, and military power. It was there that the elite worked and lived. There were considerable differences, not only in power and influence but also in culture, dress, and language, between those who lived in the city and those residing in the villages and rural towns. Thus, even on islands as small as Malta and Gozo there existed a fairly pronounced cleavage between town and country.

The division between town and country still exists, but it is much less pronounced than it was fifty years ago. As we shall see, many persons from the village work in the city. They travel to and from their place of work daily. Though the Maltese and, to a lesser extent the Gozitan, villagers are partially industrialized, agriculture, however, still continues to play an important subsidiary role. Many work during the day as unskilled and semiskilled industrial laborers and return to till their lands and tend their animals at night. Almost half the population lives outside the conurbation centering on Valletta. These people still see a considerable difference between themselves and the city dwellers, and especially between themselves and the upper and middle classes living in Sliema, the smart suburb which has grown up next to Valletta during the last fifty years.

This is the place to emphasize once again that this study deals with rural rather than urban Malta.

A bird's-eye view of Hal-Farrug. (Courtesy H. M. S. Falcon. Crown copyright reserved.)

Farrug

THE SETTING.   Hal-Farrug, the village on which this study is focused, is situated in the southern half of Malta. It is more or less at the center of the villages and towns there, none of which are more than 2 miles from its central square or *pjazza*. Farrug, with a population of 1290, is slightly smaller than most of its neighbors. Though it may be smaller, its structural characteristics are very much the same, as is its appearance. The flat-roofed limestone houses are grouped close together along the winding little streets which radiate from and circle around the central square in front of the parish church. All but 7 of the 244 households live in the built-up area of the village. These compact settlements, separated from similar communities by open fields, are characteristic of most southern European societies. The village square in front of the church is the focal point of the religious, social, political, and economic life of each village. Local citizens endeavor to live as close to it as they can. Throughout the Mediterranean the community with the highest prestige is the city, and each of the rural villages and towns in its own way imitates the crowded urban settlement pattern. The ideal of a country home far from the crowded streets of village or town—and also from the square, from neighbors, shops, clubs, and church—so familiar to the north European or North American, is totally foreign to the south European. Farrug reflects this concentrated concentric settlement pattern. The more important local institutions are clustered near the center of the town. Most of Farrug's nine shops and five cafes, as well as the police station, the two band clubs, the football club, the Catholic Action center, and the little chapel of the Annunciation, not to mention the parish church, are located on the main square or on the streets immediately adjacent to it. People like their village and they like to live in it. The Maltese in general and the villagers in particular are sociable. Though they often get on each other's nerves, and long-standing arguments between neighbors are not only common but also sometimes very bitter, they like living near each other.

The houses, in general, are roomy. Each is built around a little courtyard and often has a small garden which provides the household with vegetables, spices, and flowers. Each family also normally has a number of chickens and rabbits, which are housed in the courtyard or on the flat roofs.

LOOKING BACK. Farrug was established as a separate parish in the year 1592. At the time, it was a farming hamlet with fifty houses scattered about the crossroads at which with the little chapel dedicated to Saint Martin was built. This was to become the center of the village. As shown in Table 1, the population of the village rose slowly, but it has more than tripled in the 375 years since its foundation. The village's growth has been far from regular. Periodic epidemics and plagues held the population in check or reduced it during long periods. For example, it declined between 1667 and 1772 because several epidemics, including the virulent plague of 1676, decimated the inhabitants of all southern villages. In fact, the little chapels of the Annunciation and Saint Nicholas, just outside the village, were built during this period to mark the final resting places of hundreds of victims of the plague. The church of Saint Nicholas is still used as the village cemetery. The chapel of the Annunciation is used now only as a meeting place for the female Catholic Action groups. There are several other little burial places for plague victims, marked only with stone crosses, in the fields surrounding Farrug.

TABLE 1
POPULATION OF FARRUG, 1592–1967[a]

Date	Population
1592	50 hearths
1667	363 people
1772	270 people
1871	509 people
1960	1293 people
1967	1290 people

[a] Source: Parish records, Miège (1848, p. 150), 1871 Census Report, and author's surveys.

The population has remained almost constant for the last twenty years. When I carried out my fieldwork in 1960, there were 1293 persons living in Farrug. Seven years later the population had decreased slightly to 1290. Increasingly, persons are emigrating from the village or moving elsewhere. There are (1960) about thirty births a year, but these are counterbalanced by an average of ten deaths and another fifteen persons or so who emigrate. Another four or five marry out of the village annually.

The event that looms largest in the memory of the older inhabitants of Farrug is their experience during World War II. To begin with, the village lost approximately one-third of its territory, including some of the most fertile agricultural land, to the Royal Air Force, which expropriated the land to build a landing strip next to the village. Although its loss seriously reduced the village's agricultural potential, for until the war it had been chiefly a farming community, the Royal Air Force paid generously for the land. Many of those who were forced to sell land in this manner invested the money paid them wisely and now derive a substantial income from the property they bought with it. Tereza Abela, for example, lost most of her dowry land to the Royal Air Force, but she has succeeded in multiplying many times over the £300 which she received for it in 1939. Not only has she been able to provide handsome dowries for her three daughters; recently she paid £20,000 (part of which was a loan secured by her suburban property holdings) for two buses and shares in the regional bus company so that her four remaining sons would not have to emigrate like their two older brothers.

Many persons had their houses destroyed during the war by enemy action, for the village was bombed repeatedly during 1940, 1941, and especially 1942. During these difficult years the villagers virtually lived underground in the many air-raid shelters they dug into the soft limestone on which the village rests. Many of the thirty-five children who were born in 1942 were, in fact, born underground in the shelters. Forty persons died that year, mostly from pneumonia and other illnesses brought about by days and nights spent in the shelters, which in winter were bitterly cold and often half-flooded.

The war brought other profound changes to the inhabitants of Farrug. It gave the men, many of whom were conscripted, an experience of discipline and the regular hours of wage labor. It also showed them the advantages of regular cash income compared to the uncertain income they had formerly derived from agriculture. Many men entered the war as farmers and emerged from it as skilled or semi-skilled industrial laborers.

For these and many other reasons, it is no wonder that Farrugin look on the war as the most important social milestone. They often remarked, "Before the war we were farmers and very poor. Now we are much better off and we are not so ignorant as before." These are more than just vague impressions. Although the first primary school was established in Farrug in 1885 and a resident schoolmaster was sent to live there, prewar education left much to be desired. Children attended school only casually for half a day, for their parents often required their help in the fields. In the survey I carried out, I found that though most of the older villagers had, indeed, been to school, few had stayed there beyond the first year or two. Many were illiterate. Compulsory education did not really begin until after the war, and full-time schooling, that is, during both mornings and afternoons, did not become reality until the Labour government took office in 1955. Now, all children are obliged to attend school all day up to the age of fourteen.

It was only after the war that the village received electricity, running water, and paved roads from the government. The sewage system was not constructed until 1963. It is not strange, therefore, that the villagers often remarked, "Before the war we were only partly civilized." During and after the war the village also became linked more directly with the wider communication network on the island. Before the war there had been only one bus a day to and from Valletta. By 1950 these had increased to five, and to twelve by 1960. Today, buses make twenty-seven round trips a day between Farrug and Valletta. Thus, it has become possible for the people of Farrug to participate actively in the economic and social life of the nation, which centers on Valletta and the Grand Harbour. Rediffusion, a wired sound-relay service, established a link with Farrug in 1948; by 1960 three out of every four households had rediffusion loudspeakers. In 1960 there were only twelve television sets in the village; there are now seventy-three (thirty percent of the households). The village is now linked via the communications network with the national political and economic framework. Though Farrug was a relatively isolated village before the war, this is certainly no longer the case today.

EARNING A LIVING. The transition from agriculturalist to industrial laborer was a gradual process. Nonetheless, if one compares the occupational structure in 1960 with the situation prevailing in 1871, the radical change that has taken place during the last century becomes apparent: The number of full-time farmers, which stood at 77 percent of the male working population in 1871, had decreased to 15 percent by 1960. The shift in the occupational structure of the village is set out in Table 2.

TABLE 2
OCCUPATIONAL CLASSES IN FARRUG, 1871 AND 1960[a]

	1871 (%)[b]	1960 (%)[c]
Professional (priest, teacher, clerk)	2	4
Skilled worker (craftsman, fitter, technician)	8	24
Service worker (soldier, policeman, waiter, driver/cabman)	11	22
Unskilled industrial laborer	2	35
Agricultural	77	15
	100	100

[a] Source: 1871 Census Report, pp. 64–107, and a survey that I conducted in December 1960.
[b] N = 176.
[c] N = 296.

This shift in the means of earning a living has brought about a profound change in the rhythm of life in the village. A century ago all but sixteen percent of the villagers worked within the limits of the village; today, seventy-four percent work outside the village. Most have little or no contact with each other at their place of work. The village is no longer the economic and social whole that it was a century ago, when the men spent the entire day in or near the village and were in much more frequent contact with each other. Three out of four men now leave the village every morning around 7:00 A.M. to return only in the late afternoon. Thus, during most of the day the village belongs to the women and the children and to the groups of older men who have retired from the economic scene and now sit gossiping on the street corners, seeking out the sun in the winter and the shade in the summer.

Nonetheless, the village still provides employment for seventy-seven (26

Digging the potato cash crop, an important source of extra income.

percent) of the men. There are two priests, three teachers, eight shopkeepers, one policeman, and one baker. Another eighteen men work in the stone quarries which surround the village. Many of these are owned by villagers. Finally, forty-four men work on a full-time basis as small farmers and cheesemakers. In addition to these full-time workers, another seventy-eight men work in the village after their return from their working day outside it. Most work as part-time farmers on their fragmented plots of land, producing potatoes and onions. These cash crops substantially supplement their incomes as drivers, mechanics, or, more usually, as unskilled industrial and construction workers. This means that just over half (52 percent) of the men of the village draw either a substantial supplement to or all of their income from the village itself.

This part-time work is very characteristic of the Maltese. Most Maltese, whether civil servants or unskilled laborers, whether they live in towns or in villages, supplement their fixed income with various other activities. These extra sources of income provide an important contribution to family budgets. They enable the Maltese to maintain a relatively high standard of living in spite of apparently low wage rates. The average income of an unskilled industrial laborer in 1960 was about £6 10s. a week. (It has increased slightly, but so has the cost of living.) Most families in Farrug spend more than that per week. This is made possible by the extra income the family earns to supplement the weekly pay packet. The family of Baskal Attard illustrates this. Baskal is an unskilled laborer who works for the Royal Air Force. He has four children, none of whom are working. The oldest girl, seventeen years' old, lives with and takes care of the eighty-year-old parents of her mother, and thus, does not tax the family budget very heavily. Baskal brings home £6 a week. He owns his own house and, thus, pays no rent, but the expenses of the family, which his wife calculated for me over a four-week period, averaged £7 1s. 10d. a week. The deficit of almost 22s. a week was made up partly by selling eggs, chickens, rabbits, and the milk of the family's two sheep. As Farrug is a fairly important center for the production of the soft cheese (*rikotta*), many families keep a few sheep to supplement their income by selling milk to the cheese manufacturers. In addition to the extra income, the Attard family derives from the sale of milk, Baskal also plants potatoes on a small piece of land his wife received as dowry. From these he can make as much as £50 in a good year, for the early Maltese potatoes are much in demand in northern Europe.

It is interesting to note that the important regular supplement to the budget derived from the sale of poultry and milk is entirely the responsibility of the women. Rosaria, Baskal's wife, does all the work connected with the sheep: She milks them, takes them out to graze, brings the milk to the cheese maker, and bargains with him when necessary. Her oldest daughter helped her with this until she went to live with her grandparents. The younger children are still too small to assist her in these chores, although they do help her keep an eye on the grazing sheep. When the children are old enough to take the sheep out by themselves, Rosaria plans to buy a few more sheep, for she will then have more hands to help her. She will thus be able to increase the family income a bit. This illustrates another important point. Among rural Maltese, especially among the humble villagers such as the Attard family, the income is still a family income, as it was in the days when most Maltese villagers derived their livelihood entirely from the fields. The Attard family is now considered to be one of the poorer families of the village, but as the children grow older and are able, in their turn, to contribute to the family budget, first through making it possible to own more sheep, but later through their wage packets, the fortunes of the family will rise sharply.

Because of the fluctuating income of the family during the life cycle of its members, and because many villagers derive a supplementary income from part-time farming and other activities, there are not great differences in standards of living between the various segments of the village population. Certainly, some families are better off than others, but because there are no representatives in the village of the upper middle class—doctors, lawyers, notaries, and old business families—there are not the tremendous social differences that one finds in many larger Maltese villages and towns. There the differences between the life style of the local doctor and notary, who often have large, sumptuously furnished houses and several cars, and that of village families such as the Attards, who have neither car nor television, and live together in a small five-room house at close quarters with their animals on £7 a week, is striking. Though Farrugin recognize differences in wealth, they see these as temporary. They look on each other as equals. Most families have their roots in Farrug or in similar, neighboring villages. All call each other by their first names and, sometimes, by their nicknames. Pietru Cardona, a teacher who spends a lot of his free time helping his mother and sisters farm, once summed this up for me with a sweeping gesture by saying, "Gerri! There are no classes here. Here we are all equal. Nobody is better than anyone else." While there may not be more than one class present in Farrug, nonetheless, as we shall see in a later chapter, there are a number of families who regard themselves, and are regarded by others, as a little more equal than others.

2

Family and Relations

MALTESE SEE THE FAMILY as the most important institution in their lives. It is thus convenient to begin our closer examination of Farrug by first studying the many families which make up the village itself. From one point of view Farrug may be regarded as a collection of families. The ideal household is composed of an elementary or nuclear family, that is, a father and mother with their unmarried children, living together in a separate house; but the reality differs considerably from this ideal. To begin with, by no means all persons marry, and not all those who do produce children. This means that the kinship groups that the anthropologist encounters are the domestic groups or households. These are often composed of one or more nuclear families or segments of nuclear families and various relatives. In Farrug, for example, out of the 244 households there were only 101 nuclear families which did not share their houses with other relatives. Another twenty-two gave accommodation to some relatives. Then there were fifty-seven households composed of nuclear families of which the children had begun to leave the house, either through emigration or marriage. There were also twenty-two households composed of the remnants of nuclear families, such as a widow and her unmarried daughter, a husband and wife all of whose children have married and left home, a widower and his sister's children, and the like. Finally, there were another forty-two households composed of miscellaneous relatives such as bachelors, or a group of unmarried brothers and sisters living together, or childless old couples, and so on.

In spite of the many various combinations of relatives which compose the households of Farrug, the nuclear family remains the normative ideal household. It is in many respects the building stone of Maltese society. This chapter examines not only the function of the family, the various roles that are played out within it, but also the way that the network of relatives which stretches out from the family is ordered. The next chapter considers how the children contract relationships with other similar families through marriage, the forces which determine where the

13

newly married couples will take up residence, and which relatives they will visit most often.

One of the themes running through these next two chapters is the influence that changes taking place in other social fields, notably in the economic field, are having on the kinship system. Another theme is that structural form and content of kin relations are not merely a reflection of the values and norms which are commonly held to govern behavior between kinsmen. Such structural form—for example, the pattern of residence after marriage—where it can be shown to exist at all, is more than likely to be the result of scores upon scores of individual choices, each of which has been influenced not only by ideal norms but also by practical exigencies related to or derived from a person's role in other fields of social activity. Simply expressed, the collective pattern of behavior, or the structural form, is a reflection of pragmatic choices made by many individuals (Barth 1966). These are choices made not only in answer to the question "What is expected of me by others in this particular situation?" but also to such questions as "What is best for me and my family?" "From which possibility will I derive the greatest benefit?" "How much can I get away with?"

The Family as a System of Roles

It is useful to begin the study of the family by examining some of the roles which are played out within it. The concept of role is, of course, borrowed from the theater. By role I mean the set of norms and expectations that are bound to a person who occupies a particular position (Banton 1965). The individual who fills this role and those to whom he plays out the role, each hold certain preconceived ideas of how he should behave. In a small face-to-face society such as Farrug, the expectations held by each party usually coincide. Sometimes, however, they do not. In such cases, conflicts are liable to arise. It will be apparent also that an individual plays several roles at the same time. A man may be father, son, and husband. These roles complement each other, but also overlap. This may give rise to tensions and frictions which sometimes are expressed as role conflicts. For example, a newly married man often finds a certain incompatibility between his roles as son, husband, and son-in-law. As a son, he is expected to visit his own mother regularly, but as a husband, he is expected to accompany his wife on her regular visits to her mother. Because, as will be shown later, the tie between mother and daughter is particularly strong, the man very often sees more of his mother-in-law than of his own mother. This can give rise to misunderstanding and friction between mother and son.

Finally, it is important to note that the roles one plays in various areas of social life are not without influence one upon another. Thus, the role which a person plays, for example, in the economic field may have a direct bearing upon roles occupied in the kinship field.

Before taking a closer look at the various roles within a family, it is well to draw attention to an important fact. Not only is the family the basic unit of Maltese society, it is also the basic unit of the Catholic Church, which, as will be seen, plays an extremely important part in Maltese social life. The Church regards the family as the principal unit of religious socialization. In the family the individual first learns the values and mission of the Church into which he is born. The family is also the primary unit of reproduction for the Church, the agency through which it replaces and increases its numbers. The family, thus, has a spiritual function; it is an organic part of the Church. For this reason the Catholic Church has protected the family by erecting around it an elaborate system of safeguards. The family roles to be described are protected by religious sanctions. By not performing a role correctly a person may be liable not only to the pressure of the public opinion which is against him but also to penance imposed by the Church's mortal representatives and, of course, to spiritual punishment after death. Because most Maltese, and certainly all Farrugin, are Roman Catholics, most of whom practice their faith devoutly, the way in which the Church defines and protects certain roles is extremely important.

The Church regards marriage as a natural contract between man and woman which Christ has raised to a sacrament.[1] The husband/father's contribution to this partnership is to provide food and shelter. Moreover, the father also has the ultimate authority in the family, to which all members are subordinate. He also represents the family to the outside world. The wife/mother's role in this sacred contractual partnership is to produce children whom she is to tend and train for the service of Christ. Thus, a woman can secure her own salvation and insure the future of the Church by acting out her role as wife and mother as defined by the Church. These are positive sanctions of great power. Because of the spiritual consequences to it of her role performance, the Church has repeatedly stressed that a woman's place is in the home, and that once she is married, she should not go out and work.

The civil code of Malta, insofar as it deals with the juridical status of the sexes, reveals the same bias in favor of men, as do the pronouncements of the Church. That this is so is not surprising: The Maltese civil code is very largely a marriage of Roman law and canon law. To a certain extent, Maltese law regards a married woman as a legal minor. Though a woman may own property, and all rights in it are vested in her: She may not give it away or sell it or otherwise dispose of it without the consent of her husband or guardian.

Upon marriage a woman enters into a contractual agreement with a man, which commits her to a set of legally sanctioned rights and obligations. In general, both partners owe each other fidelity, support, and assistance. The civil code notes that the duties of the husband are to act as head of the household, and to protect, receive, and maintain his wife. The wife is bound to take her husband's surname, to obey, to live with, and to follow him. She is also obliged to contribute to his maintenance if he is incapacitated.

Finally, we must note that though divorce does not exist in Malta, the civil code provides that if one of the partners does not meet his or her contractual marriage obligations, the other can demand a legal separation. This involves a separation of bed and board, the return of the dowry property to the wife, and the division of the property and goods which the couple acquired during their marriage. The separated partners may not remarry. A legal separation is thus the ultimate step that a wife can take to protect herself against the abuse by her husband of his super-

---

[1] Documentation for this section is furnished in Boissevain 1967.

ordinate position. In Farrug there are three cases of husbands and wives who live separately. The national average is 130 legal separations as against approximately 2000 marriages a year.

As noted, the husband is supposed to provide the income. His wife has responsibility for the interior of the home: the cleaning, cooking, marketing, the care of the children, and the care of the household animals. The income she earns from this supplements her husband's income. As we have seen, this extra income often makes the difference between solvency and debt for the families of the poor unskilled industrial laborers. The wife usually controls the spending of her husband's income as well.

When the husband is at home, he does not normally help with the household chores, though he will often bounce the younger children on his knee and in other ways keep them amused when his wife is very busy. In farm families, the wife and some of the other women of the family form part of the economic unit which operates under the authority and supervision of the husband/father. Each member contributes in his or her own way: Women often help with the harvesting and planting, as do the children.

Though there is a division of labor in the home, the tasks are not exclusive. When his wife is incapacitated, a husband can and does do the cooking and marketing and cares for the children, aided sometimes but not always by the wife's sisters or younger brothers, who may live nearby. For example, Leonard, our neighbor in Farrug, the husband of Tereza Abela's youngest daughter and a policeman with the services, took care of his two small children while his wife was in the hospital having her third baby in as many years. He also readied the house for the large baptis-

The woman's domain: the interior courtyard of a village house.

mal party with which he greeted his wife upon her return after three days in the hospital. During all the cooking, baby tending, shopping, dusting, and washing that this involved, he received only token assistance from her married sister, who lived next door, and four unmarried brothers, who lived farther up the same street and with whom he was on excellent terms.

In principle, the husband exercises the formal authority in the household, but in fact, the actual authority is very often in the hands of his wife. Moreover, as Malta becomes progressively more industrialized, fewer households operate exclusively as agricultural production units under the authority of the husband and father. This means that his authority is undermined, for he no longer has wife, sons, and daughters working under him. His dependents now often contribute more to the family purse—which is administered by his wife—than he; but if his relative power in the household is decreasing, that of his wife has remained constant, and, thus, in relative terms it may even have increased. This is the case where the wife makes an important contribution to the family budget.

In this respect it is interesting to compare the relative authority in their own families of Tereza Abela and Angela, her daughter married to Leonard, the policeman. Tereza is an extremely powerful woman both in body and in spirit. Moreover, as has been pointed out, she is wealthy personally, having manipulated her dowry property into what is regarded as a small fortune by village standards. Her husband is an unskilled laborer who works with the government Refuse Disposal Department. At home she is clearly in charge, and her children, including her married daughters, respect her and greatly fear her anger. Although her husband and the three sons still living at home are working, it is she who exercises the greatest economic power within the family. At home Tereza commands, and her husband, although by no means a weak little man, is kindhearted and has apparently given up disputing this fact.

The authority Tereza exercises in her own household may be compared with that which her daughter Angela wields in hers. Angela makes no contribution to the family purse. She and her three children are completely supported by the wages her husband receives and the extra income he earns buying rabbits and eggs locally and selling them in Floriana. She has all she can do to manage her house and tend to her three children, who have come in as many years. When we left the village in 1961, she was pregnant again. She is very clearly subordinate to her husband. The difference in the power that Tereza and Angela wield in their respective households may be partly explained by differences in character, but I suggest that equally if not more important is the difference in the economic roles they play in their families. Tereza plays an important if not dominant economic role. This carries over into her role performance as wife and mother, where she tends to dominate. Angela's role as wife is not affected by her economic role. In both she is subordinate to her husband, although as her children grow older, her domestic empire (decisions and responsibilities in her role as mother) will also increase. She will also have more free time away from her demanding infants, which she will probably devote to economic activities (raising livestock). These will increase her authority in her household.

The bond between mother and daughter is important in most societies. It is particularly strong where there is a marked separation between the social world of men and women. In Malta mothers and unmarried daughters spend much time in each other's company. The daughter helps in the house, performs domestic chores for her mother, and grows up under her close supervision. A pattern of mutual aid and companionship is established from an early age. After marriage this companionship continues, though it changes in character. If the newly married and yet childless couple live nearby, the daughter can still come and take care of her younger sisters and brothers, and help with the domestic chores and marketing. There is no sharp break in the routine of service and companionship, though the young wife begins to divide her time between her natal home and her own.

The real change in the flow of service comes when the married daughter has her first child. The mother then comes to the assistance of her daughter by providing advice and helping with housekeeping and marketing, and later by looking after her grandchild while her daughter sees to these chores herself. This is an important source of aid, for few can afford domestic servants. This is the ideal type of relationship between mother and daughter, whether they are from the country or the city, whether from farming or industrial families; but the degree to which the ideal relationship can be realized depends upon several variables. The most important of these is the place of residence. When the newly married couple lives in the same village as the wife's mother, the relations they have developed can continue; but when the couple lives at a distance, or nearer to the husband's family, certain obstacles arise. Mother and daughter cannot communicate as frequently as in the past. Moreover, the obligations of the husband to his mother as well as those of the wife to her husband's mother pull in opposite directions.

A son's link with his mother is also very close. She has cared for him, spoiled him, and done many services for him at home; but when he is six, he begins to move out from under the direct control of his mother to enter the all-boy world of school and catechism. He begins to follow his father and older brothers about the village in the early evening. At the age of ten or twelve boys begin to help the men with the elaborate decoration of the village for the annual festa of the patron saint. Later, when he has finished school and begun to work, he will spend the entire day away from home, returning after work only for supper and to change his clothes, before leaving again to join peers in the square or the clubs. His sister, in contrast, spends both her working day and her leisure time at home or visiting maternal relatives with her mother. While there is a strong bond of affection between mother and son, it is not characterized by the intimate companionship and degree of mutual services that exist between mother and daughter.

The relation between father and son, when the son is young, is characterized by a strong sentimental attachment; but this changes as the son gets older and the father begins to play a more authoritative role. Though the mother exercises authority consistently over all her younger children, her sons fall increasingly under the authority of their father as they move into the male world. This is especially marked in farming families, where sons work directly under the authority of their fathers; but there is not the same degree of companionship as between mother and daughter in their domestic working arrangement. As the son matures, his relation with his father is often competitive. However, the authoritarian relation between the father/employer and son/farm worker is modified in families in which father and son work as wage earners. Moreover, because sons have increasingly more education than their fathers, they are able to obtain more prestigeful employment and to make a greater contribution to the family budget. It thus becomes more difficult for the son to submit to the traditionally heavy domestic authority of his father, isolated from other role relations and unsupported by economic sanctions.

The father/daughter role is characterized by affection while the daughter is young. This changes to one of very considerable social distance as the daughter reaches puberty. As long as the girl behaves according to the canons of modesty advocated by Church and public opinion and gives the neighbors no cause to gossip, they get on very well. There is no basis for friction in the economic and jural fields, as there is between father and son.

The relation between brothers and sisters is also an affectionate one. Mutual services pass between the two. There is a good deal of companionship where brother and sister are near each other in age. This is absent where there is a considerable difference of age. The younger one is expected to perform little services, such as carrying messages, baby tending, and so on, for the older one. There is frequent contact and affection. The same is true of the relation between two brothers or two sisters. In Malta married brothers are not expected to share a house or cooperate economically as is the case in many Mediterranean societies. Nonetheless, they are expected to remain on friendly terms. When the parents are living they meet often at their house, for children, even though married and living in another village or parish, are expected to come at least once a week to visit their parents, and as property considerations are very important, they like to maintain contact with the parents so that they shall not be forgotten in the family will. The inheritance, however, more than any other single factor, drives a deep wedge between brothers and sisters. There are at least four groups of brothers and sisters in Farrug who are not on speaking terms. In each case I traced the origins of the dispute back to a conflict over inheritance. Lawyers had been called in and they had ended by taking each other to court. A well-known example in Farrug is the case of the Abela family. Tereza and her fourteen brothers and sisters fought each other physically and legally over their father's inheritance. In the ensuing battles, Tereza and her own large family defended her interests legally and physically with great skill and verve. In fact, most of them have been to court either to sue or to testify against their rivals for everything from personal injury resulting from physical assault to swearing and throwing dirty water in the street. Even the younger first cousins had been to the police to report each other for selling cheese and fruit without a license, throwing stones, riding bicycles without proper lights, and so on. Now, only two sisters out of this large family are on speaking terms with each other.

More—Distant Relatives

The Maltese have large families and reckon kin relationships equally through males and females. Each person is thus at the center of a wide network of blood relatives or cognates, and relatives by marriage, or affines. The Maltese make a linguistic distinction between these two classes of relatives. The first they call the *qraba* (derived from the word for near or close, *qrib*). The relatives by marriage are called *l-imhalltin* (from the word *thallat,* to be mixed). One of the objects of this study is to build a model of behavior which will indicate how persons who are related to each other in a certain way will behave toward each other. We must ask, therefore, how relatives in each category behave toward each other, and how they behave toward persons from a different category. What sort of rights and obligations exist between children of brothers and sisters? Do these correspond to the rights and obligations between a person and the first cousin of his wife, for example? It is also interesting to ask if there is a difference in the rights and obligations that exist between a person and the relatives of his father, on the one hand, and those of his mother, on the other. Finally, it is important to determine whether there are permanent groups of kinsmen who share collective rights and obligations toward each other. Such groups exist in many of the societies studied by anthropologists, including some relatively close neighbors of Malta such as many of the Balkan societies, Turkey, and North Africa.

BLOOD RELATIVES. The villagers of Farrug live surrounded by relatives of all sorts. A person feels closest to his blood relatives, the cognates of his father and mother. Sometimes these are collectively referred to as one's *razza,* or people who are of one blood, *ta'demm wiehed;* but all the relatives of one *razza* do not have equal importance. A person normally makes a distinction between his "immediate family" (*qraba tal-familja*), his "close relatives" (*qraba ta'gewwa*), and his "distant relatives" (*qraba fil-boghod*). A man's immediate family, or *qraba tal-familja,* normally consists of his parents, his brothers and sisters, and their children. Each category is extended as a matter of courtesy to the wives and husbands of the brothers and sisters. This set of relatives normally see each other at least once a week and share a certain number of rights and obligations. In general, they are expected to help each other, but the obligation and expectations to give and receive services diminish as the social distance between them increases. They visit each other in case of illness, take care of each other's children, and help each other in many little ways. They also give each other financial aid. Moreover, they are expected to invite each other to betrothal, wedding, and baptismal parties and to their annual village feasts if they live elsewhere. Finally, they are expected to help in times of crisis, and to attend each other's funerals. The assistance rendered or refused is not forgotten, and the help that can be expected is largely determined by past performances.

The close relatives, that is, those who are designated as *qraba ta'gewwa,* include not only relatives designated as *tal-familja* but also grandparents, parents' brothers and sisters and their wives (uncles and aunts), and their children (first cousins). Many people place grandparents among their closest relatives, and designate them as *tal-familja.* Relatives in this category, although they are close relatives who see a great deal of each other, do not expect to be invited to the more intimate family celebrations such as betrothals and baptisms, although they frequently are. It is difficult to draw hard and fast lines with regard to these customs because they depend a good deal upon the social position of the persons involved. For example, families in Sliema and some of the larger villages make enormous celebrations out of baptismal and engagement parties. They invite distant relatives as well as nonrelated friends to these. This has not been the custom in Farrug, though it often happens that a favorite cousin is invited to a baptismal party, but these customs are changing rapidly, and some Farrugin are beginning to copy these urban customs.

The *qraba ta'gewwa* expect to be invited to wedding feasts. Their counter obligation, if they are invited, is to send a present and attend the reception if possible. It is viewed with disfavor if they do not call on each other in case of grave illness. They are expected to be present at each other's funerals. They should also give help to each other if in a position to do so. In the event, however, that a member of a person's immediate family, such as a brother, and a close relative, such as a first cousin, both ask for the same service or favor, a man is, of course, expected to favor his brother over his cousin. These relatives in general see each other several times a year and sometimes a good deal more frequently, for they all have other relatives in common. They often entertain each other during the annual feast of the village patron saint. For example, Pietru, the schoolteacher, was invited by his mother's sister, who lives in Qrendi, a neighboring village, to celebrate the feast of Santa Maria, the village's patron, with her family. Arriving about noon, he shared the big festa meal with them and stayed until about 10:00 P.M. There was a special relation between this aunt and his mother, for the aunt, who is childless, had adopted Pietru's youngest sister. Pietru sees very little of his mother's two brothers in Qrendi, one of whom is a very wealthy contractor. When we passed one of them in the street on the eve of the feast—which I attended with Pietru—they merely nodded to each other and exchanged a few words. Later, Pietru said that his uncle is a miser. He had not sent a wedding present when Pietru's other sister was married.

A person's distant relatives, his *qraba fil-boghod,* include the brothers and sisters of grandparents, the great grandparents, and their descendants. These may include second cousins and even third cousins, if they are known. A person normally has no formal contact with this set, but he recognizes the relationship if it is known to him. He says that they *jigu minn xulxin,* that they are related. On several occasions I was told that a person to whom an informant was speaking was a second or a third cousin. This certainly does not mean that a person knows all his more distant relatives, especially if they live outside his own parish. Although Maltese villages are close together and transportation is continually improving, geographical distance unquestionably generates social distance. Such relatives may, of course, become friends, in which case they would be invited to wedding feasts, and asked to come to visit during the village's annual festa. Such invitations are not expected between distant relatives. There are, however, no hard and fast rules regarding the frontier of the category of distant relatives or *qraba fil-boghod.* The relatives of a person which may be placed in this category are not determined by rule but rather by social (and geographical) distance in combination with personal likes and dislikes.

The limits of what we may call effective kinship, that is, where fairly clearly defined rights and obligations regarding services and help exist, extend normally to the category of the *qraba ta'gewwa.* That is, to grandparents, uncles and aunts, and first cousins. The limits of the category of distant relatives, the *qraba fil-boghod,* extend normally one degree farther, and include second cousins, but between known relatives in this category no more than a feeling of relatedness exists. I do not know if, once relationship is known, and all other things are equal—and they seldom are when dealing with people—second cousins will favor each other over nonrelatives. I should suspect they would. The English proverb "Blood is thicker than water" has a Maltese counterpart: "Blood will never become poison" (*Id-demm qatt ma jsir semm*). Pietru and his sisters went to visit a maternal second cousin (mother's brother's son's son) in a neighboring village when they heard that he had been badly beaten in a fight. Pietru said he did this because he wanted to show the young man, who had just come back from Australia, that he could count on his relatives in case of trouble.

It should have become clear by now that these sets of kin are not fixed or bounded groups. First, a person is relatively free to invite whom he wishes to any given ceremony. Second, these kin sets are not enduring groups that have other corporate characteristics such as common property and rights and obligations that are shared equally by all members. Physical as well as genealogical distance combine with sentiment to determine the actual relatives who are placed in these rough categories by an individual. Thus, a person may be on closer terms with his second cousin who lives next door to him than with a first cousin living in another village. Normally, however, certain relatives expect to be invited to particular ceremonies, and failure to invite them leads to friction, or may be a reflection of an existing conflict. Thus, when Tereza Abela's son Carmel married, not one of his many maternal relatives was present. His mother has fourteen brothers and sisters, who, in turn, have forty-three children of his generation. In other words, there were at least fifty-seven relatives who might have shown up had they been invited. They were not invited, however, because Tereza Abela, her husband, and children had fought with all her brothers and sisters and were not on speaking terms with them.

Kin relations are, thus, flexible. The relatively close relations which are supposed to exist between brothers and sisters as well as between their children are not infrequently ruptured by violent quarrels over inheritance. Long-dormant links, however, can be activated and manipulated for special purposes, such as to arrange introductions to persons with political or economic influence. Once a kin relationship is made known, it establishes a special tie between the two parties and preferential treatment often follows; for kin are expected to help each other if they can.

RELATIVES BY MARRIAGE. Upon marriage, a person extends the range of his immediate family to include the corresponding set of his spouse. A married person has, of course, two sets of affines, or relatives by marriage: those persons who are married to his own blood relatives, and the blood relatives of his wife. Thus, the wife of a father's brother becomes an honorary aunt, a *zija tar-rispett*. She is addressed and referred to as though she were a blood relative: *zija*, aunt, if the affective relation is close, otherwise, by her Christian name. Such honorary relatives are always included in invitations given to the blood relatives, but relatives of these honorary relatives are not considered as relatives. Thus, while Pietru addresses and refers to his father's brother's wife, whom he sees often, for they live opposite each other, as *Zija Victoria,* and shows affection for her, he shows none whatsoever for her various relatives who also live nearby. He does not regard them as his relatives.

In the same way that the spouses of one's cognates are regarded as honorary relatives, so a person is regarded by the family of his wife as an honorary relative.

He is identified and invited with her. In fact, it often happens that strong friendships develop between brothers-in-law. Pietru and Censu, the husband of his sister, are firm friends and help each other in many ways. Each is the person to whom the other turns first if he needs help in repairing his house, for harvesting, and even in a financial crisis. They help each other for the sake of the relatives they share, a wife/sister and a mother-in-law/mother. They are *haten*, brothers-in-law.

It is worth noting that blood relatives never assemble on any occasion without the presence of some of their relatives by marriage. This is partly because affines are closely identified with the set of blood relatives, but it is also because they may perform special functions that cannot be performed by the blood relatives themselves. Thus, in financial discussions, men, though not cognates, must legally represent women who are. For example, when Pietru's mother's brothers and sisters met to divide the property left by his maternal grandmother, Pietru went along to represent the interests of his mother and sister. While all his mother's brothers were there, his mother's sister had brought along her husband. The wives of the uncles were not present. The discussion regarding the inheritance, incidentally, reached a conclusion that satisfied everyone. The relatives did not have to call in an outsider to divide the estate, nor did they have to take each other to court to resolve differences of opinion. This smooth settlement was made possible primarily because Pietru's maternal grandparents had made it a point while they were alive to distribute most of their property equally among their children through dowry and gifts.

Thus, although it is possible to make theoretical distinctions between categories of blood relatives and affines, these distinctions are not so easily drawn in practice. The categories of relatives form a *network* of relations and not separate groups. A person chooses a set of relatives out of his total network of relatives. He maintains more intimate contact with these and shares with them rights and obligations which flow forth from this intimacy. Some of these persons may be members of his immediate family, close relatives or more distant relatives. Some of his most intimate contacts may be not with blood relatives but with affines.

Mother's and Father's Relatives

The way a woman's role is defined by Catholic moralists and by the legal statutes of Malta, together with the customary segregation of men from women, give an apparent masculine bias to the social structure in Malta. One might expect that the Maltese kinship system, though bilateral—kin relations are calculated equally through both men and women—would favor the relatives of the father. This is the case in most Mediterranean societies. At first sight it also appears to be so in Malta. Father right is supported by both the Church and the civil code; a wife is obliged to obey and follow her husband and to take his name. Moreover, children inherit the father's surname and, usually, his nickname. In fact, however, the kinship system in Malta has a matrilateral bias. That is, the mother's relatives are favored over those of the father. This derives principally from the strength of the tie between mother and daughter. The strength of this bond influences the frequency of contacts with kinsmen outside the elementary family and also, as will be seen in the following chapter, the pattern of residence. Naturally, where a couple settles nearer the relatives of one of the partners, these are usually visited more frequently; but even where a couple establishes its residence more or less at an equal distance from both sets of relatives, those of the wife are favored, though most couples try to maintain a balance. The male informants with whom I discussed this all said that while they tried to maintain regular contact with their own parents, they saw a good deal more of their wife's near and distant relatives. This not infrequently leads to conflicts with their own mothers, who resented the transfer of attention.

Since the strength of the mother-daughter tie skews visiting patterns in favor of the wife's relatives, it follows that if a couple shares a house, it is most often with the wife's relatives. Very often, the relative is a widowed mother or father, or a bachelor brother. The wife's brother is favored over the husband's brother. This is logical, for the incest prohibition ensures that there will be no competition between her brother and her husband for her sexual favors, as might well be the case between the husband and his brother, should the latter share the house with them. In Farrug thirty married couples lived with their relatives. Of these, nineteen lived with the relatives of the wife, and eleven with those of the husband.

The matrilateral skew of the kinship structure also affects the attitude of children toward their maternal and paternal kin. As the family tends to see more of the mother's kin than those of the father, the children grow up having greater contact with their maternal relatives. The aunts and uncles on the mother's side are among the favored relatives, as are their maternal cousins. Of the uncles, the mother's brother nearest her own age is usually a favorite. As already noted, the mother's brother may live with the family, but even where he does not, he is a special relative for the children and, conversely, they are privileged children from among his many nephews and nieces. Often, this special relationship dates from when the children were first born and their parents lived with the maternal grandmother. This was certainly the case with Pietru, who was unmarried and still lived at home in 1960. His married sister lived next door. He was, thus, the first uncle that his sister's children ever met, and they, in turn, were the first children to call him uncle. I can remember once watching his little nephew Carmelo edging into a dense crowd in the *pjazza* to see the festa procession. He asked his father to carry him so that he could see better. When he refused he sought out Pietru and in a few moments I saw him perched high on his uncle's shoulder. During the many hours I spent in the company of his uncle I never saw him speak harshly to the boy or even reproach him. Though I saw the boy and Censu, his father, together much less frequently, upon several occasions Censu was obliged to speak sharply to him, for living practically in the same house with doting maternal relatives had spoiled the boy and made him rather naughty. The father disciplines his son; the uncles usually spoil him. Children make a special point of seeking out their maternal uncles on New Year's day, in order to receive the annual New Year's gift of money (*l-Istrina*).

Very often, the maternal uncle is also the boy's godfather, and then there is privileged behavior, for a godfather is expected to show his *filjozz* special consideration. When the maternal uncle remains unmarried, he often becomes a powerful patron. I know of a number of priests, for example, who have helped to educate their sisters' children and in other ways give them powerful help and protection.

The mother's brother is not the only maternal kinsman favored. The mater-

nal grandmother has an especially warm place in her heart for her daughter's children. Her son, as we have seen, is often involved with his wife's relatives to the
point that he begins to see less of his own mother than of his mother-in-law. This is
the case with Censu, Pietru's sister's husband, who is from the neighboring village
of Mqabba. He lives right next door to his wife's relatives. His children do not
have the frequent contact with their paternal grandmother that they have with their
mother's mother, their favorite *nanna*. In fact, little Carmelo and his sister see their
paternal grandmother only once or twice a month. The preference of a woman for
her daughter's children is embodied forcefully in the proverb: "Your daughter's son
you cuddle in your lap, and you kick your son's son" (*Bin it-tifla tilqghu f'higrek, u
bin it-tifel taghtih b'riglek*).

The mother-daughter link is one of the most significant kin relationships in
Malta. Its influence on visiting patterns, living arrangements, and the contact between more-distant relatives has been suggested. In brief, I have argued that this tie
articulates the Maltese kinship structure. Its importance will be observed again when
marriage residence is examined in the next chapter.

3

Marriage

MARRIAGE IN MALTA may be regarded as an arrangement between two groups of persons. In face-to-face communities such as Farrug, and those studied by most anthropologists, marriage, while a contract between two *individuals,* is, in fact, a matter of immediate concern to two *groups of persons,* the families of the bride and groom. Marriage is the culmination of a series of steps which have placed the principal actors in contact with each other's close relatives. It is also a transaction which involved gifts and countergifts between the two groups of relatives. In Malta this takes place in the form of a dowry, the property that the family of the bride settles upon her at the time of her marriage. Prestige can be increased or lost through marriage. All parties are keenly aware of this. Thus, marriage can also be seen as a competitive game played between the two groups concerned. That is, the players have certain goals or prizes which they hope to win. These may often be reduced to *prestige:* prestige derived from a high dowry, marriage into a wealthier or socially more prominent family, the beauty and character of the bride, the intelligence and education of the son-in-law, and so on. Often, pragmatic considerations play a role, and a marriage may be manipulated to yield important political or economic benefits. The players also follow a set of rules. These concern not only the type of persons with whom one may play the game (usually from same social category) and those with whom one may not (usually from other social categories) but also the moves that may be made by the various players. Within the rules of the game there is considerable latitude for maneuvering; in short, for the expression of the self-interest which motivates the players. Marriage is, thus, the outcome of a series of choices motivated by self-interest that the interested parties have made within certain culturally defined limits.

The Rules of the Game

Marriage was seen to be an arrangement between persons in which the Church has a great interest. It was noted that certain canonical safeguards are erected about it. These include limits to the type of persons who may marry. The first of these limitations is the incest prohibition. That is, sexual relations between members of one's immediate family are prohibited by the Church, the law, and by public opinion. Quite obviously, if such sexual relations are not possible, neither is marriage, at least in Malta.

Not only are sexual relations between members of the same immediate family forbidden but the Church also forbids a person to marry uncles, aunts, or cousins out to the third degree. Neither may marriages take place between a person or his children and his godchildren. The Church, however, does grant dispensations, and a relatively large number of cousins are married each year. In Farrug there were four sets of first cousins who had married and as many second cousins. There are several reasons for concluding such marriages. The first is related to prestige. Two of the sets of first cousins who married in Farrug were members of the two families with the highest prestige in the village. They could not contract marriages outside their qraba ta' gewwa within the village without marrying social inferiors. The second reason is that marriages between first cousins can be economically beneficial: Such marriages provide a means of keeping the property of the grandparents intact. Finally, cousin marriages occur because there is considerable social contact between first cousins, who can often wander in and out of each others houses and have an opportunity of becoming far better acquainted with each other than do unrelated persons who are continually chaperoned. Thus, cousins also marry because they like each other and because they know each other better than they do other persons of their age of the opposite sex; but dispensations for such marriages are not easy to obtain and are expensive. Cousin marriages are thought to be somehow not quite proper.

The restrictions placed upon marriages between kinsmen tend to direct the choice of a marriage partner outside the group of kinsmen. In small villages this means that the number of eligible persons within the village is restricted. There is no rule which obliges a person to marry within or outside the village. Consequently, many seek their partners outside the village. In fact, 37 percent of the native Farrugin still resident in the village have married outsiders. Many more have married out of the village. Their numbers are increasing as communication improves. The proportion of marriages with outsiders is somewhat higher than in most Maltese villages because, among other reasons, Farrug itself is smaller than most, and the choice within the village is, therefore, more restricted.

Besides the formal rules of the Church as to which persons may not marry, there is another social factor which operates to limit the field of choice: distance in geographical, social, and moral terms. Before a marriage is contracted the two young people and their respective families must be able to meet each other. They must also be able to obtain trustworthy information about each other. This they can only do through their network of intimate relatives and close personal friends. Persons have more opportunities of meeting suitable members of the opposite sex, and of finding out detailed information about them, among those who live relatively near them. People thus tend to choose partners who live near them. Of the 234 marriages recorded involving native-born Farrugin of which one of the partners was still living in the village, 172 were either contracted within the village (105) or the six neighboring villages (67). The rest found their spouses outside the district. Thus, seven persons out of ten have sought and found their marriage partners within a radius of about one mile or twenty-five minutes by foot. This same preference for the district is also shown by those Farrugin who have married and moved outside the village.

Social distance is also an important consideration. In the game of courstship and marriage each side tries to gain prestige. This means, effectively, that a person tries to marry within or above his or her own social prestige group or class. Failure to do so results in a loss of prestige for self and family, and a corresponding increase in prestige for the spouse and his or her family. If neither side is to lose, the marriage must be between social equals. This means that the field of choice is again narrowed down. One must seek a spouse who comes from approximately the same social background, whose family is of at least the same economic level. The implications of this will be examined shortly and in the following chapter. One way to resolve the problem, as we have seen, is to marry a close relative.

Another important consideration is that the future spouse must have a good moral character. This is particularly important for girls, for the reputation of a man is not quite so vulnerable on moral grounds. Relatives and close friends play an important role in advising whether this is the case. A girl's moral standing and general reputation are determined by public opinion. If public opinion, in the form of reports and comments gathered by one's relatives and close friends, is favorable to the girl, then she is acceptable on moral grounds. If the reports are unfavorable, then to contract a marriage with the girl and to continue living in the same community in which this unfavorable opinion is held results in a loss of prestige for the man and his family. In such cases the couple may choose to move into a new community in which this reputation is not known. People of Farrug often observed that "a good cow is sold at home" (Baqra tajba tinbieh f'pajjizha). This points to the importance of a girl's reputation and moral standing. The implication is clear that if a man marries a girl from another village he is getting someone rejected by others who know her better. Therefore, to be safe one should try to marry as near to home as possible.

In addition to the factors already described, personal characteristics also tend to restrict the field of choice. It is important to underline once again that in Catholic Malta the partners cannot divorce and remarry, as is possible in so many other societies, both primitive and modern. Each wants to be sure of the other. The ideal qualities the man looks for in his wife are that she be submissive and willing to accept his authority, pleasant to live with, religious, industrious, healthy, and capable of bearing children. Personal beauty is also a factor. The ideal girl should not be too dark. Boys smilingly describe dusky girls as dangerous: "Turkish" girls. I was told that such a girl is very passionate. She is nice to know before marriage, but dangerous afterwards. Her sexual appetite knows no bounds. It was implied she would either exhaust her husband, be unfaithful to him, or both. One of Pietru's cousins is unmarried at the age of 30. I thought this strange, as she comes from a reasonably good family, she is industrious, reasonably well educated, and—I thought—quite attractive. I was told that she is unmarried because she is ugly. She is too dark. I was not able to verify if this darkness relates only to her physical coloring, or, as I suspect, also to her moral reputation.

Beauty and personality as well as geographical and social proximity all enter into the choice of a marriage partner. Though many of these factors which have been discussed are implicit rather than explicit, they are known to the persons seeking marriage partners. They thus operate to limit effectively the field from within which a man or woman seeks a marriage partner. Though these limits are not as rigidly defined as they are in India, for example, where a person is obliged to marry within his caste, their effect within a bounded society such as Malta is not unsimilar. Young men and women thus make a choice from within a limited field of possible marriage partners; but their parents have the power of veto. Their final decision is taken at the time the dowry is discussed. This property settlement is a matter upon which the prestige of both groups depends.

Property Considerations

The dowry, legally speaking, is the property which the wife, or any other persons on her behalf, brings to the husband at the time of the marriage. Technically, it is to assist the husband to support the burdens of marriage. In fact, it is a property settlement in anticipation of their death that the parents of the wife make on their daughter to help her to achieve a comfortable life, and an economically viable marriage, especially in its early years. Its second avowed purpose is to give the daughter a measure of economic support should she separate from her husband. It can also be seen as gift which parents make, through their daughter, to their grandchildren. A more detailed analysis of the dowry system can give a number of insights into the status of married women.

To begin with, an unmarried woman has a legal right to a dowry; if this is not given, she can appeal to the courts to sue those responsible on her behalf. If the parents or guardians are dead or incapacitated, the responsibility for the dowry falls upon the grandparents, then upon the parents' brothers and sisters. Only if these lineal ascendants in both lines are dead or otherwise incapacitated does the responsibility for providing a dowry fall upon a girl's brothers. Thus, brothers and sisters have true rights of maintenance against each other only if the lineal ascendants to the second degree are dead. Though the girl has a right to a dowry, however, her father can legally refuse one if she chooses to marry someone of whom he disapproves. His disapproval, however, cannot be because he dislikes the occupation, social position, class, or character of the intended spouse. It must be based upon his public misconduct. This, of course, is difficult to establish unless such misconduct has already brought the future groom into contact with the courts. In fact, however, if the parents of either the boy or the girl object to the marriage, they raise difficulties over the dowry. The groom's family will complain that it is inadequate or that the quality of the furniture is poor. The bride's family simply offers a sum that they know will be unacceptable. Many marriages are prevented because there is disagreement over the marriage payments.

The dowry is arranged at the time the parents meet to discuss the marriage. Normally, so I was told, the parents of the groom call upon those of the girl. Although I did not ask systematically about this point, in the three cases with which I was more or less personally involved, only the mother of the groom called on the parents of the girl. Few persons, apart from the wealthy urban elite, bother about a marriage contract (*kitba taz-zwieg*), though it is the right of the girl's family to do so. The advantage of a contract is that it specifies the dowry property. Thus, there can be no argument as to the amount involved should the court call for a restitution of the dowry in the event of a legal separation at a later date.

The form that the dowry must take is not specified. It may consist of clothes, jewelry, cash, furniture, kitchen appliances, a house, or land. The dowry can be provided from the property of either the father or the mother, or from both. A girl will often work for her dowry or a portion of it. The exact form the dowry takes is not as important as the amount it is worth.

There is, however, no crushing moral obligation to provide a sumptuous dowry, as there appears to be in rural Greece (Friedl 1963). Many girls get married with a dowry consisting only of an inexpensive bedroom suite and their personal clothes. Considerable prestige is derived, however, from being able to display a lavish dowry, and the higher one moves up the socioeconomic ladder, the more important a social weapon the dowry becomes in the competition for prestige and status.

As noted, the dowry is inalienable. Although the rights of usufruct (use) and management are vested in the husband, it remains the property of the wife. The husband cannot sell the immovable property without obtaining his wife's written consent, although that of her family is not required. If the woman has no children, the dowry property passes back to her parental family, unless she wills it to some other person, such as her husband. If her children die before she does, however, the dowry is passed on to their children, her grandchildren.

The dowry must also be regarded as an anticipated portion of the inheritance. There is equal inheritance in Malta, and daughters inherit equally with sons. The amount of the dowry is calculated as part of the family estate and is deducted from that portion the daughter receives when the estate is finally divided after the death of the last parent. The principle of equality of heirs means that if one parent dies, the property is divided equally, with the children and the wife getting an equal share. The surviving spouse naturally still retains his or her property. Even if there is a will, the offspring have a right to one-third of the estate, in the case of four or less children, and to one-half if there are more than five. The surviving spouse has the usufruct of the balance of the estate. A will is often used to exclude gifts previously made from the estate to be divided among the heirs. Thus, if one son gets an expensive education and another none, the latter may get a gift of money, the father noting in his will that these gifts are to be exempted from "collation," that they are not to be considered part of the inheritable estate.

A dying man is often under considerable pressure to change his will to exempt such gifts from collation. I collected a number of macabre stories in Farrug as well as other villages about the lengths to which children, as well as the administrators of certain ecclesiastical foundations, occasionally went in order to arrange for last-minute bequests.

The Process of Marriage

While the families of bride and groom are keenly interested in the match, the initial choice of a suitable partner lies with the young people concerned. Individual choice has apparently always been of importance, although the opportunity to choose was at one time considerably more restricted than it is today, for men and women, especially of marriageable age, were more segregated from each other in the past than they are now. Even today, there are persons whose chances of marriage within the circle of their own acquaintances, or to persons they are likely to meet, is almost nil. For example, widows, widowers, and extremely ugly persons, or those who suffer from some form of physical, mental or moral defect are often unable to marry without outside assistance. The institution of the marriage broker or *huttaba* exists in Malta to help people who wish to get married to come in contact with each other. Although the services of the *huttaba* were formerly much more sought after than they are today, I noted several cases where the couples concerned had been introduced by a marriage broker. In Farrug two men had found their wives in Gozo with the help of a *huttaba*. One was our next door neighbor, the paternal uncle of Tereza Abela, Ganni Gafà.

This is the story that I heard from our neighbors; Ganni himself was not forthcoming on the subject. Some five years before we moved to the village Ganni's wife had died. He was childless and he found it very difficult to live alone and tend his house and his animals as well as his crops. He wanted to remarry. He asked a *huttaba* to find him a good sturdy farming girl who could take care of his house, help in the fields and, most of all, who could provide him with long-sought-after children. He told the *huttaba* that he was wealthy and just fifty years old. Within a few weeks the *huttaba* located a Gozitan woman of thirty-five, from a farming family, who was prepared to move to Hal-Farrug as the wife of this wealthy middle-aged widower. The arrangements for the marriage were speedily made and the couple was introduced to each other. The woman found, instead of the promised wealthy middle-aged farmer, an old man of seventy who, she was later to learn, was famous in the village for his miserly and antisocial conduct. He, in turn, found not the thirty-five-year-old farm maiden promised by the *huttaba,* but a tough, very solid woman of fifty-five, many years beyond child-bearing age.

The villagers laugh when they tell the story and remark that neither got a bargain. Both deserved what they got for their dishonesty. The only one to make a profit on the transaction was the *huttaba,* who received her commission. Ganni and his Gozitan bride were married and have lived together since, but in considerable tension. Ganni's bride is sharp-tongued. She not only fights with him but also with all her neighbors, and especially with Ganni's grandnieces, the daughters of Tereza Abela, who live opposite her.

Turning now to the notion that a marriage develops gradually, one can, in fact, distinguish a number of steps in the process of courtship. The first is the meeting. Most manage this without the help of a *huttaba*. The traditional place for young Maltese of marriageable age to meet is during the village festa. There, groups of girls meet and talk with groups of boys out of the sight of their parents in the milling crowds in the village square. Many of the married couples I interviewed in Farrug had met at village festas. Many also meet at wedding feasts, where young people are thrown together and, nowadays, even dance together. I have already pointed to the privileged contact that cousins have.

In recent years the nightly stroll up and down Kingsway has become one of the most important places where village boys meets girls. Kingsway, the main street of Valletta, is closed to motor traffic from 6:00 to 10:00 P.M. To this street stream young men and women from all the villages in Malta. There, they stroll up and down for hours in groups of two's and three's, talking and flirting. Around nine o'clock, however, everyone begins to move toward the bus terminals at King's Gate and Castile Square, where the girls take the last bus that gets them home before the ten o'clock deadline which most parents impose.

After boy and girl have met, they begin to make appointments to see each other, secretly, either in the less-frequented lanes outside the village or, more probably, in Kingsway, though many fathers will not allow their daughters to go there every night. The couple are now "speaking" to each other, but their parents do not know this, officially. Boys and girls are not supposed to be in each other's company until they are officially engaged. This informal period of secret contact goes on, usually, for two to three months, and sometimes even longer. If it goes on much longer, the parents of the girl, although they probably know she is seeing someone, may have it called to their attention publicly by a neighbor. In that case the parents must act to preserve the honor and dignity of the family and the image of parental authority. They will have to break it up. When Leonard was courting Angela, Tereza Abela's youngest daughter, they used to meet while she was herding the family sheep near the airstrip that he was guarding. They were usually separated by a high wire fence. After two months of these secret meetings Angela, who was extremely frightened of what her mother would do to her if she found out, prevailed upon Leonard to call on her family.

The next step in courtship takes place when the young man calls upon the girl's father and asks permission to "speak" to her; but sometimes before this he tries to determine through an intermediary, often his mother, who explains the boy's interests to the mother of the girl, what her father's reaction will be. If the boy is from a different parish, the mother sends out messages through her personal network to see if the young man's character, moral standing, and economic position are suitable. She may also ask the boy's parish priest. If the messages that come back are positive, the father gives his consent and a meeting is arranged between the parents, who are often represented only by the two mothers. The girl and boy are then officially introduced to each other and, so I have been told, must pretend that they do not know each other. They go to the side of the room and talk while the parents discuss the details of the marriage settlement. What are his prospects? What has he saved? What property can he bring in to the marriage? These must be balanced against the dowry which the girl's family will send with her. This is a tense moment for the young couple, for it often happens that their plans are shattered by the failure of their parents to reach an agreement on these matters. If all goes well, the young man is given permission to call on the girl. After this they are never supposed to be alone, although this custom too is changing rapidly. The young man may now call on the girl in her house and, accompanied by a relative or friend, publicly take her out walking, to the cinema or, if he has a car, out driving. They are now officially engaged and may speak to each other openly. Their engagement may last many years until they find a suitable house and accumulate the household goods to furnish it.

Another step has been added in recent years. This is the formal blessing of the engagement rings and the betrothal party for intimate relatives that takes place around it. This is a custom that has come to the village from the urban upper classes in general, and from Sliema in particular. Older married couples in Farrug had not had their rings blessed. A number of the couples who were engaged while I was in the village had this ceremony performed. Each invited the very closest relative, those I have characterized as *tal-familja,* to witness the blessing of the rings by a priest who was either a relative or a good friend of the family. This in a certain sense is merely a gloss on the official meeting between the parents of the two parties, for all the important details have been settled and the couple are officially "speaking" when this ceremony takes place.[1]

The next big event is the marriage ceremony. Banns are read and posted in the parishes of both boy and girl three consecutive Sundays before the marriage. The wedding, according to Church regulations, must take place in the parish of the bride and be performed by her parish priest. Very often, however, it is performed, with the permission of the parish priest, by a priest who is a relative or a good friend of the family. Important contacts of the parents of the bride or groom are invited to act as witnesses to the wedding. As the wedding to a lesser or greater extent is a public display that serves as a claim to higher prestige within the village, the more important the witness the greater the chance of gaining prestige.

After the wedding ceremony the bride and groom, accompanied by their closest relatives and the witnesses, walk to the place where the reception is held. In Farrug wedding receptions are usually held in one of the two band clubs; whether it is the club of Saint Martin or Saint Rocco depends upon the factional allegiance of the couple. The party walks through the square and the main streets, which are usually lined with people curious to see the way the bride and the wedding party are turned out. As soon as the couple enter the reception hall and are seated in the place of honor on a raised dais, the guests begin a mad scramble for seating. Most of the guests are women and children, but many men come and stand along the edges. Waiters begin serving refreshments immediately. During the three to four hours that the wedding reception lasts tray upon tray of drinks and plates of sandwiches, sweetmeats, biscuits, and sweets are brought in in an abundant stream. There are several interruptions in the eating and drinking. The first comes when the bride and groom are whisked away to the photographer in Hamrun to have their official wedding portraits taken. Another comes when they pose for the traditional

---

[1] I learned on my return to Farrug during the summer of 1967 that the scale of these engagement parties has greatly increased since 1960. Now, many nonrelatives are invited, and the guests give presents to the girl.

The wedding reception of the baker's daughter.

dancing picture. Not one of the many brides to whose weddings I was kindly invited knew how to dance. Nor did most of the guests. Nonetheless, the efforts of a jazz orchestra hired for the occasion forms an ear splitting background to the festivities.

The not inconsiderable costs of the reception are born by the bride's family. The families of both the bride and groom wish to have as elaborate and large a feast and as many guests as possible, for the prestige of both families is actively involved, but as the family of the bride must pay for the affair, a limiting factor is introduced. In villages such as Farrug a large wedding in a band club or a special reception hall, now increasingly common, may cost well over £100. The reception of the baker's daughter, the biggest I saw in Farrug, cost nearly £200. Among the Sliema elite and those aspiring to be so considered wedding costs often reach astronomical proportions. A good city friend calculated that his wedding reception, which lasted three hours, cost his wife's family £2 a minute. He stressed that it was a relatively average affair. He had attended weddings that cost three times as much.

After the wedding ceremony the couple usually leaves for a honeymoon trip. When the baker's daughter was married, she and her husband left the reception in the Saint Martin band club in an enormous hired limousine. Their car roared out of the village at top speed, its tires screeching as it swung through the twisting streets, but after five minutes they returned quietly to the bride's house on the other side of the square. There they took off their wedding finery and invited me to take pictures of the sumptuous display of dowry furniture and wedding presents. They spent the first night in the bride's house, where they subsequently lived. The next day they left for a four-day honeymoon in a small hotel at St. Paul's Bay.

The final step in the marriage process takes place when the couple sets up its own household. This sometimes consists of only a separate room in the house of one of their parents, but this is always regarded as a temporary arrangement, no matter how long it lasts. The first child arrives, if all is well, during the first year of the marriage. These then are the usual steps leading up to a village marriage. An extended example will help to illustrate them more clearly.

The Courtship of Carmel Abela

Though the details of the courtship and marriage of Carmel Abela, the first of Tereza Abela's sons to marry, do not conform in all respects to the normative model just sketched, they are offered as a case history of the way in which one village marriage came about. Carmel recounted the story of his courtship while helping me wash my car in the garage that I rented from his mother. He told me that he met Anna, his bride-to-be, on Monday, May 1, 1960. He had been at his sister's house in Qrendi helping his brother-in-law add a new room to their house. Anna, who lived opposite his sister's house, happened to come in and borrow something. Carmel said he looked at her out of the corner of his eye, but was too shy to say anything. After she left his brother-in-law teased him and jokingly offered him £100 if he would marry the girl. Two days later Carmel again went to help his brother-in-law and again caught sight of Anna. The following day again he went to Qrendi, this time to help his brother-in-law dig potatoes. He saw Anna again, but he did not speak to her. He said he was still too shy. In the meantime his sister had noticed Carmel's interest in the girl and had discretely established that Anna was also interested. The following Sunday Carmel's sister by chance met Anna's mother, a widow, who lived with her own mother. They met at a wedding reception. She mentioned that her brother was interested in Anna. Anna's mother said she did not believe her. The following Tuesday his sister chanced to meet Anna's mother in the street. Again, she mentioned her brother's interest in her daughter. Anna's mother replied that she had to think about it. Actually, she was already busy finding out all she could about Carmel and his family.

On Thursday Carmel went to his sister's and impatiently learned that though she had twice mentioned his interest, Anna's mother had not given a definite reply. Carmel, who has a very abrupt and to-the-point nature, told his sister to ask the mother over. His sister crossed the road and invited Anna's mother for a visit. When she arrived, Carmel abruptly told her of his interest in Anna. He stressed that he could have met her daughter secretly, but that he much preferred to tell her and obtain her permission. He was very anxious to be able to call on her. He did not want to wait any longer. Anna's mother replied that he must wait a little longer. The impatient suitor told her to ask his acquaintances about his character. She would find that he was hard-working and honest. He had nothing to hide.

The following Saturday, May 14, Anna's mother and Carmel's sister went by bus from Qrendi to Hal-Farrug to meet Tereza. Apparently, everything went well. Anna's mother explained that her daughter would have a dowry worth about £300. Tereza, in turn, pointed out that her son had a good job—he was then an electrician with the dockyard—and would get a substantial inheritance of land and money. It is interesting to note that the entire discussion between the two families was conducted by the women, for Carmel's father was not yet back from work. Carmel came home from work shortly after noon. He told me he was astounded to find Anna's mother talking to his mother.

Carmel then suggested that he take the family car (which was seldom used and kept shrouded in dust sheets) and drive Anna's mother and his sister back to Qrendi. He quickly sent word through one of his younger brothers to his brother-in-law Leonard, his sister Angela's husband, to come quickly. Leonard when he came, suggested that he accompany the party back to Qrendi. Carmel was very grateful for the moral support, for by that time he was exceedingly nervous.

When they returned to Qrendi, Leonard told Carmel that that was the time to meet and speak to Anna. About fifteen minutes later mother and daughter came to Carmel's sister's house. Carmel and Anna were then officially introduced to each other. They sat together on a small sofa and spoke together for the first time.

Another fourteen days had to pass before Anna's mother would allow Carmel to call at her house. She was afraid of what her own mother would say of this whirlwind courtship. She needed time to prepare the way with the old woman. During this time he also had to promise not to meet Anna outside his sister's house, for her mother was worried about what the neighbors and the grandmother would say if the two met publicly before it was officially known that they were engaged. A month after he saw her for the first time, Carmel was finally able to call on Anna regularly at her house.

Anna and Carmel were married in Qrendi on August 6, 1961. The reception was held in the parish hall. The wedding sponsors were Carmel's father's sister and her husband. This aunt, a dressmaker, also made Anna's wedding dress. There were about 150 people present at the reception. Most of the guests were the bride's relatives. From Carmel's side only his mother and father, his brothers and sisters, his brothers-in-law, his sisters' children, and several of his paternal cousins were present. With the exception of the wife of one of his first cousins, not one of his many maternal relatives appeared. This was because, as previously noted, his family had quarreled with his fourteen maternal uncles and aunts over the inheritance of his maternal grandfather. After the wedding Carmel and Anna went for a two-day honeymoon to a hotel in the north of Malta.

They set up their own household immediately, for they were able to move into a flat in one of the houses that Tereza owned in Farrug. They were fortunate, for the place of residence provides one of the most difficult problems for a newly married couple in overpopulated Malta.

Marriage Residence

Kinship is not just an abstract concept or a set of rules. It is what real people who are related think and do. Marriage residence patterns are, thus, an indication of the relative importance different related persons attach to each other. As already noted, ideally, each newly married couple in Malta sets up housekeeping apart from their parents. There are, of course, several possibilities, all other things being equal. A husband and wife can establish their residence nearer the parents of the husband, nearer those of the wife, or equidistant from both. The consequences of this choice are particularly apparent if the partners come from different villages. The figures from Farrug, taken at face value, do not indicate that any particular choice is favored. As shown in Table 3, of the 234 marriages for which I gathered data in Farrug, 105 are or were composed of Farrugin who married within the village and 123 of Farrugin who married outsiders. Of these last, 61 are men, and 62 women. Exactly half, thus, chose to live nearer the relatives of the wife, and half nearer those of the husband. Yet when each of these couples married they faced the problem of where to live.

One of the objects of any analysis is to try to build a model which makes it possible to predict what will happen. An analysis should, thus, lead the reader to an understanding of the relative importance of the factors which the people themselves take into consideration when they make their choices. Once these factors are understood, he should be able to make decisions which approximate those of the people being studied. The cumulative total of these decisions is what, in fact, shapes the structural pattern or form which anthropologists try to describe. What then are the factors which influence the decisions regarding marriage residence that result in the unremarkable pattern already noted? Soon after I arrived in Farrug, I began asking informants about marriage residence. There are no explicitly formulated rules on the subject, and I was answered with a wealth of often conflicting information. These were statements about the often contradictory factors that govern the choice of residence. Almost invariably, informants quoted the proverb "A good cow is sold at home," thus pointing to the importance attached to a girl's reputation. Many noted that traditionally, the wife went with the husband, as she is obliged to by law. All noted that because of the housing shortage, people today went wherever they found suitable accommodations. They also noted that more often than not if they had to live with in-laws, they chose the wife's parents because a woman often quarreled with her mother-in-law. At this point they would quote another proverb: "The husband's mother is cooked in a pan" (*Omm ir-ragel moqlija fit-tagen*). Others went on to note the importance of the help a young wife could expect from her mother during child-birth. These maintained she would thus move to be near her mother. In the same breath they observed that if the husband were a farmer the couple would settle in his village. Some said that a man usually moves to his wife's village so that she can be near her relatives. All said that it was not possible to talk about a rule: marriage residence depended upon many things.

Where husband and wife are from the same village and there is suitable housing available there, the choice presents no problem, but a choice has to be made when, as is increasingly the case, the bride and groom are from different villages. As has been observed, many factors enter into this choice. The most important of these, leaving suitable housing aside, appear to be the services and help a new couple can expect from their respective relatives and the occupation of the husband. It is, obviously, important for the couple to live in the husband's village when his occupation is in his village, as it is if he is a local shopkeeper, artisan, or a farmer with land and livestock. This economic factor becomes less important, however, if the husband is an industrial laborer, for the transportation from most parts of Malta into the central industrial area around the Grand Harbour is excellent. What remains constant, however, is the fund of good will and the important services a woman may expect from her immediate relatives, and from her mother in particular. This is especially important in the difficult early years of marriage, when the many children are still small and need a great deal of attention. Maltese families are very large and the age difference between successive children is often no more than ten months or a year. Seen pragmatically, therefore, the help and psychological support that a wife receives from living near her kin must be balanced against the inconvenience for the husband of perhaps slightly longer trips to work and to visit his own family. It is important in this respect that a man resident in his wife's village can continue to participate in the social life of his native village, and many do (Boissevain 1965, p. 37). In contrast, a woman's social life is bound up primarily in her family and with her relatives; it is not possible for her to continue this if she lives in her husband's village, for she is not as free to travel as her husband is.

Given these factors, it is possible to formulate a predictive proposition that reads something like this: *If a marriage is contracted between persons from two different villages and the man works outside his own village, then he will tend to live in the village of his wife.* Its corollary is: *when the husband works insiae his own village, then his wife will tend to move there to join him.* However, considering the large number of variables and that we are also dealing with human beings, we must not expect a very clear pattern. What do the data from Farrug in fact indicate?

As shown in Table 3, while the total number of men and women who have married into the village is the same, fifty-six out of the sixty-one men (92 percent) who have married into the village are industrial laborers who work outside the village. This supports our proposition. At first sight its corollary does not fare so well, for only twenty-six out of sixty-two men (42 percent) whose wives married into the village actually work in the village. They are mainly farmers and quarry operatives.

TABLE 3
MARRIAGE RESIDENCE AND PLACE OF WORK IN FARRUG[a]

| Husband's Place of Work | Type of Marriage | | | | Both from Outside Village | Grand Total |
	Both from Village	Wife from Village	Husband from Village	Total		
Inside parish	47	5	26	78	1	79
Outside parish	58	56	36	150	5	155
	105	61	62	228	6	234

$df = 2; \chi^2 = 24.69; p < 0.001.$

[a] There seems to be a highly significant relation between place of work and type of marriage. Expected frequencies in the column "both from outside" are too low to include this column in the χ^2 (statistical significance) test. This is not serious since the argument does not pertain to this type of marriage.

However, of the thirty-six apparent exceptions to our corollary—the local men who work outside the village and whose wives are outsiders—no less than fifteen have important land and livestock holdings in the village with which they substantially supplement their wages. Thus corrected, forty-one of the sixty-one men (66 percent) whose wives have married into the village also work in the village. This substantiates the corollary. The remaining twenty-one exceptions can be explained for the most part by the availability of housing in Farrug. This is also why Carmel Abela and his bride settled in the village.

There thus appears to be an important connection between place of work and marriage residence, but is this also true of other villages? Can we generalize? As place of work is closely related to type of occupation—a farmer works in his village, an industrial laborer outside it—we can formulate a further and more easily testable proposition and a corollary: *Where there are more farmers than industrial laborers, there are also more outside women married into a village; but where there are substantially more industrial laborers than farmers, the number of in-marrying men is greater.* While I have not been able to make a study of other villages as detailed as my study of Farrug, this residence pattern appears to be reflected in the proportion of outside women as compared to men resident in a sample of seven Maltese villages and three Gozitan villages I investigated. In the still very agricultural Gozitan villages, 61 percent of the outsiders are women, compared to only 46 percent for the semi-industrialized Maltese villages. These data are summarized in Table 4. This is, of course, only a crude index, for the facts that more men than

TABLE 4
ADULTS BORN OUTSIDE THEIR PLACE OF RESIDENCE
COMPARED TO FARMING POPULATION[a,b]

	Number of Adults in Sample	Farmers	Outsiders	Female Outsiders
Maltese villages	5473	18%	861 (15.7%)	397 = 46% of 861*
Gozitan villages	1330	57%	188 (14.1%)	115 = 61% of 188**
Farrug	575 (total adult population)	21%	(23 %)	57%

* $z = -2.24$; $p = 0.0125$.
** $z = 2.99$; $p = 0.0014$.

[a] In Gozitan villages, where there are a high percentage of farmers, one expects a high proportion of female outsiders. This was tested statistically with the binomial test. The proportion of female outsiders (61% out of all outsiders) proved to be significantly higher than the 50% expected if the proportion of farmers had no influence on the sex ratio. The corollary—where there is a lower proportion of farmers there is a lower ratio of outside women—appears to be significant, though at a lower level.
[b] *Source:* This table was compiled from data made available to me by the principal government electoral officer in 1961 from a random sample drawn from seven Maltese villages (Zebbug, Gharghur, Gudja, Mosta, Qrendi, Dingli, and Zurrieq) and three Gozitan villages (Qala, Xaghra, and Gharb). The percentage of farmers in these villages was calculated from *1957 Census: Report on Economic Activities,* pp. 40–43. The same sources were used for the data for Farrug.

women emigrate and that women live longer than men distorts the proportions somewhat, as does the relative availability of housing. For example, in Farrug, which was very badly damaged during the war, most of the houses were enlarged after the war with funds from the War Damage Commission. This partly accounts for the relatively high proportion of outsiders in the village. In combination with the possibilities for local work to supplement wages, it also accounts for the relatively high percentage of female outsiders.

The shift in the pattern of marriage residence is another way in which the increasing industrialization of Malta is affecting kinship patterns. The matrilateral bias pointed to in the previous chapter, which derives from the strength of the tie between mother and daughter, would appear to be becoming more pronounced as Malta becomes more industrialized. The strength of the tie between mother and daughter influences the quality of the contacts with kinsmen outside the elementary family. Moreover, as has been shown in this chapter, where the husband works away from his place of residence, as is increasingly the case, married couples tend to settle nearer the wife's mother and, thus, to see even more of the wife's relatives. Their children, therefore, have more intimate relations and more frequent contact with their maternal kin than with the relatives of their father. There appears to be a clear relation between economic factors and the actual form kinship relations assume. Malta is moving forward rapidly along the road to industrialization, and it would seem that the relative importance given to mothers' over fathers' kinsmen will also continue to increase. In Malta this does not seem to be just a working-class phenomenon, as it is, for example, in London (see Bott 1957; Young and Willmott 1957). I have observed much the same pattern, although admittedly not yet very systematically, among the urban white-collar workers. It is an interesting result of industrialization in a small, bounded society.

4

Social Differences

Sex Differences

THE MOST IMPORTANT SOCIAL DIFFERENCE which cuts through Maltese society is that of sex. The religious and legal bases upon which this distinction rests have already been noted in the section dealing with the respective roles of husband and wife. The Church attaches great importance to the woman's role: She bears and educates children, and, thus, replenishes and increases the human and spiritual capital of the Church. In spite of their importance, women are regarded as subordinate to men, whom they must obey and follow.

The Maltese civil code reflects the teaching of the Church on this matter. The civil code regards a married woman as a legal minor who is not able to administer her own property. The teachings of the Church and the civil code of Malta reflect and help propagate the belief that women are inherently inferior to men. This inferiority is seen as a logical consequence of her moral weakness. Man leads and woman follows, man is strong and woman is weak. According to the Bible, it was woman's weakness which brought about the fall from paradise. This is the rationale advanced by the people of Farrug for the superior position of men and for the social barriers which segregate men and women in virtually every field of Maltese social life, although this outlook, as so much else is changing very rapidly.

The segregation of the sexes and the division of labor within the household was examined in Chapter 2. There, it was observed that the man is the titular head of the family. In public he wields the power in the family. In actual fact the situation is often otherwise. Although the man holds the formal authority, the day-to-day authority over children and household, in short, over all matters that concern the family, is exercised by the woman. Within the household a division of labor exists, but the line dividing male from female tasks within the family is not rigid.

Outside the household, however, the social line between the world of men and women becomes clearer and less flexible. This is the area of the men. Until recently, the costume worn in public by women in villages such as Farrug physically hid them from the eyes of men. The traditional Maltese *ghonnella,* or *faldetta,* a black cape one side of which is stiffened and worn over the head, renders the wearer completely shapeless and, thus, sexless. Up to World War II, the *ghonnella* was generally worn by women in Farrug whenever they left their houses. Now, only a few of the older women wear it to church.

The traditional place of women is at home; that of men, in the field and market place. Maltese village women have always helped their men with agricultural activities. The important economic contribution to the family budget of women such as Rosaria Attard and Tereza Abela has been stressed, but economic activities carried out at considerable distances from Farrug have traditionally been the exclusive domain of men. Comparatively few women in the village work. In 1960, for example, out of the 396 women over fifteen years' old, only 60 (15 percent) were economically active. Just under half (28) worked outside the village. Only seven of the working women were married, and all but one of those worked within the parish boundaries either in agriculture or as shopkeepers. Most of the girls who work outside the village work as hospital attendants or maids, though more and more are beginning to find employment as factory workers.[1]

The social line that segregates men from women runs through many other areas of social activity. In Farrug, as in other villages, girls and boys go to separate classes at school. Men and women sit apart from each other in church. All formal associations are rigidly segregated along sex lines. Women do not come in to the football club or the two band clubs except on special occasions such as the annual festas. There are separate sections for men and women and youths and girls in each of the parish associations.

In fact, one can distinguish a certain geographical separation of the sexes in the village. The area of the village around the parish church and the small square and the streets leading into it are the territory of the men, when they are in the village. Here are located the clubs and wine shops which are their particular preserves. Moreover, men of various ages often congregate in small groups on the sidewalk outside these clubs or on the street between them. The center of the village, the *pjazza,* is, thus, a male area. In fact, women and girls, when they have to pass through this area in the late afternoon or evening, after the men are home, do so rapidly and often in two's. They don't linger there. Their area is located away from the center, on their doorsteps or in their houses and in the numerous little grocery and notion shops, run, for the most part, by women; there, they meet with relatives and friends. During the long, hot summer evenings girls and married women often move out of the village in small groups to stroll along the little country lanes in search of cool air. Thus, the physical location of persons and their movements in the village and outside it are strongly influenced by their sex. This important line of social cleavage runs through all aspects of Maltese social organization. It is a basic structural principle.

---

[1] The number of unmarried working women has now risen to 118. Eight out of ten (eighty-seven) of these are working outside the village. The sharp increase in the number of working women and rise in the standard of living in the village made possible by their wages are the changes which struck me most forcefully during my return visit in 1967.

Nicknames

Each family in Farrug is a distinct social group and each has its own nickname. Persons may also have individual nicknames. These nicknames are social labels that serve to identify and fix the distinct social personality of the person or group to which they are affixed. The Maltese word for nickname is *laqam* (from graft, *tlaqqam*). A nickname is given to an individual or to a family by the village. The village also changes them.

The nicknames in Farrug also serve a practical purpose. In most Maltese villages there are a limited number of surnames in common use. In fact, there are only fifty-nine surnames represented among Farrug's 244 households. No less than fifty-five households have the surname Farrugia. Ten of the men of these families are called Martin, after the patron saint of the village. There are almost twice as many younger Martin Farrugia's. Thus, the combination of Christian name and family name is simply not sufficient to distinguish persons, for too many have the same name. There are at least 130 nicknames in use now. They provide a much clearer and more personal means of identification than do surnames.

Persons in the village are known by their first name plus their family nickname. Although each, of course, also has a surname, they are used rarely. Only the police, schoolteachers, and the parish priest, and a few wise old men, know the surnames of all the families. In contrast to the surrounding European countries, where the use of nicknames in the rural areas is also widespread, Maltese very often use the nickname as a term of address. In Sicilian the word for nickname is *'nguria,* which means insult, and many of the nicknames are insults. They point to weaknesses of character or body of the persons and families they designate. In Sicily it is a grave offense to use a person's nickname in his presence. The same is true in Spain (Pitt-Rivers 1954, p. 168). This is not the case in Malta.

Most of the nicknames used in Farrug are rather harmless. Where they do refer to a weakness, they are good humored rather than malicious. Some of the well-known Farrug nicknames are *Cinaklu* (Christ's last supper), *Borom* (pots), *Tewmi* (twin), *Kwattru* (four), *Coqqu* (cassock). The origin of these names has been lost. A hobby of many men in Farrug is catching birds with clapnets and several derive their nicknames from birds, such as *Gardill* (greenfinch) and *Summiena* (quail). The nicknames of others are derived from their bodily peculiarities or those of an ancestor. Thus, *Hahaj* (from a deep laugh), *Body* (a name often given to very small men), or *Combus* (heavily built). Another family the men of which are very dark, tough, and hairy received the nickname *Garilla* (Gorilla); but many of the nicknames have no literal meaning to either the persons concerned or their neighbors who use them. Most of the nicknames used in Farrug fall into this category. Some of the best known of these are *Kexkux, Zinnu,* and *Singes.* There are, of course, many more nicknames, a few of which are rather rude. In all I collected 150 nicknames in Farrug, including 20 that have gone out of use.

Most nicknames are composed of the noun plus the preposition "of" (*ta*). These are combined with the Christian name. Thus, the name becomes Nardu *Tas-Singes* or Ganni *Tat-Tewmi* or Toni *Tal-Hahaj* and Zeppi *Tal-Garilla,* indicating that the names are at least two generations old. The person who receives the nick-name is referred to by the definite article plus the name. Thus, the name becomes *Iz-Zinnu* and *Ic-Coqqu*. Children usually inherit the nickname of their fathers. Though sometimes the village ignores the father's nickname and the children are called by their mother's nickname. Nonetheless, the official documents which ask for nicknames require the nickname of the father's family.

It sometimes happens, however, that the village decides to change a nick-name. Often, this is because the person concerned has done something unusual or something that somehow strikes the imagination, and the name sticks. Nardu *Il-Marokk,* for example, received his nickname when he was a very small boy. His fa-ther's family nickname is *Tal-Kexkuxa,* although he is now called *Ic-Cappa.* When I asked Nardu if he had acquired the nickname because he had been to Morocco, he laughed. He replied that though he had emigrated to Canada for three and a half days—it was winter and he returned home quickly when he found no work—he had never been to Morocco. His story was that when he was a baby his parents used to take him out to the fields while they worked. They would put him in the shade of a stone wall or a carob tree. Once, he dirtied himself so thoroughly that his father exclaimed that he was as dirty as a "bull from Morocco." The nickname stuck to him. His children are designated as *Tal-Marokk,* but his brothers and their children are called *Tac-Cappa.*

A woman, although she has her own family nickname, is very often known by the name of her husband after her marriage. Thus, the wife of *Iz-Zinnu,* though a *Tas-Singes* by birth, is now called *Zinnuwa.* My own nickname in the village, *Gerri,* was derived from my Christian name. My wife was called *Gerrija.* Since ev-erybody in the village is known by either his first name or a nickname or both, this was the way in which we were designated as well. As far as linguistic forms of address and reference are concerned, Farrug appears to be a community of equals.

Sources of Prestige

Although the people of Farrug are quick to tell you that there are no impor-tant distinctions between them, that they are all from the village and, hence, are all equal, there are, in fact, differences of prestige or *fama* between them. There is a consensus of opinion regarding prestige. Some families have more and some less. It is a commodity in short supply and greatly in demand. There is, thus, competition for prestige; everyone cannot occupy the highest rungs of the prestige ladder. What are the factors and qualities which affect prestige? Some of these are education, oc-cupation, wealth, rank, family, moral and religious standing, degree of urban so-phistication, and behavior, but none of these alone can determine a person's position on the prestige ladder. All must be taken together. A person's social standing, his prestige ranking, is their sum total.

Education is a source of prestige of considerable importance. Education pro-vides the key to good employment and upward social mobility. Today, it is not enough to have an elementary school education. Although comparatively few had even this a generation ago, everyone now is obliged to remain in school until the age of fourteen. To stand a chance for the highly prized white-collar positions with the government or senior technical posts with the services, a secondary education is necessary. An ever increasing number of families are now trying to push their children through the secondary schools. One family even succeeded in sending a daughter to the Royal University of Malta, where she is studying pharmacy, but this is relatively unusual, and very few Farrug families aspire this high. Mathematics and English occupy an important place in the examinations to the civil service and Dockyard Technical College. This means a secondary-school education. In 1960, twenty-one boys and five girls were enrolled in the secondary schools. Most were in private schools run by religious orders, for the entrance examinations to the free government secondary schools were beyond the training and intellectual capacity of all but five boys and two girls.[1] Education is, thus, a means to an end. The end is employment which gives high prestige. As such, it is highly valued.

There is considerable difference in the social prestige ascribed to various occupations. Nonmanual occupations have the highest prestige, manual occupations the lowest. The free professions—the priest, doctor, lawyer, architect, chemist, notary—are at the top; the farmer is at the bottom. In many respects a government clerical officer is at the other end of the scale from the farmer. The civil servant has a steady, relatively easy job with a good cash income and a comfortable pension at the end. He also has ready access to influential persons in the government. His is a life of security and relative independence. The farmer, in contrast, has been looked down upon for centuries. He represents the traditional life of dependence: dependence upon the weather, the market, the *pitkal* or middleman for cash advances, the letter writer, and the patron through whom established authority must always be contacted.

The professional and the farmer represent the two poles in the hierarchy of occupations in the villages. They also represent the two poles of the continuum town-country, city-village. Where professionals live in the villages, they represent the city and the culture of the urban elite. They are not wholly of the village; the social networks in which they move extend far beyond their village. More often than not doctors, lawyers, and architects leave their villages to live in the town, usually in Sliema. They do this for social as well as professional reasons. Many are married to city girls who look upon life in a small village as common and rustic, and, therefore, unpleasant. In the town the professions also have a far greater field from which to draw their professional clientele. Living in the town gives them prestige. Many, however, although they now reside officially in town, maintain offices in the villages, where they see clients several times a week.

There are now no doctors or lawyers resident in Farrug, though in the past at least two Farrugin became doctors. Both moved out of the village, and both are long since dead. The local elite consists of priests, teachers, and clerks, but one has only to glance again at Table 1 to get a picture of the socioeconomic classes in Farrug. During the last forty years education and wage labor have presented the farmer with the means of escaping from his dependence, from the exhausting labor in his

---

[1] Education is another field in which rapid advances have been made. There are now twenty-seven boys and eighteen girls in secondary schools, of whom twenty-one boys and all the girls are in government schools.

rocky fields, and from the low social status which his occupation has given him and his family. Where he has had the opportunity, he has been quick to turn his back on the traditional occupation of his forefathers. The sharp reduction in the number of farmers in Hal-Farrug bears eloquent witness to this. However, the agricultural past, as already mentioned, is still very close to most Farrugin; many are also part-time farmers. There is a slowly growing proportion of nonindustrial white-collar workers in Farrug. The heads of only three of the twelve white-collar households are themselves descendants of white-collar workers. One, Victor Azzopardi, the teacher and sacristan, is the son of a former headmaster. Two are descendants of a police sergeant. The others, including the three other teachers, are the sons of craftsmen and farmers. Together, they form the core of the local elite.

Wealth is another factor which can give prestige. A person's social standing is measured more by how he spends his money than how much wealth he has. Wealth can thus be used to achieve social prestige. It can be used to acquire education, with which considerable prestige can be obtained. Wealth can also be used to gain economic power. This also gives prestige. Finally, it can be used, crudely expressed, to buy prestige and social standing. By giving generously to the collections that the parish priest organizes, by presenting lavish gifts to the Church, by contributing heavily to the festa-organizing committee, and by dowering and marrying off one's daughters in great style, a person acquires prestige. The memory of the village is very short, and there are few written records. Those records that exist deal mostly with the Church. Of the persons who lived in Farrug a hundred or so years ago only the names of persons who contributed heavily to the church are remembered. One, a skilled mason and contractor, gave generously of his time, talent, and wealth to build the twin towers of the Farrug parish church. The other, a wealthy feed merchant, gave the parish church the red damask tapestries which are still used to cover its walls during important feasts. His picture hangs in the sacristy of the church.

Wealth alone, of course, is not sufficient to give high social prestige. There are a number of very wealthy families in Farrug. Some earned their wealth as black marketeers during the war. Others, such as Tereza Abela, have invested wisely the compensation they received from the government for war damage to their houses and land. A number have stone quarries from which they earn considerable profit. Most of these persons live in small, sparsely furnished houses, dress badly, and have had little or no formal education. Most have not yet begun to use their wealth to acquire prestige. Several, however, will undoubtedly gain prestige through their children, who are being given educational opportunities that not all can afford.

Certain prestige is derived by holding high office in the village's various formal associations: the two band clubs, the football club, and the church groups. The rank of secretary or president in these associations confers prestige. However, such high rank is also a reflection of prestige which they already have. This is particularly true of the associations in which all have an interest, such as the two band clubs. These organize the annual festas of Saint Martin, the village patron, and Saint Rocco, his rival. The secretary of the Saint Martin band club, a skilled stonemason and small contractor, is a man of modest means and education. In his role as secretary, he represents the club and its members to other clubs and to the government. It also gives him certain authority over other persons when they are acting in their roles as members of the club. This gives him prestige and standing in the village. The Saint Martin club is the most active band club and upon occasion represents the entire village to the outside world, but the secretary does not have the polish necessary to represent the club at all times. If speeches are called for, he is all but tongue-tied.

The ceremonial head of the Saint Martin band club is Toni Damato, a well-to-do bachelor with a secondary school education. He is in charge of the district office of the Department of Labor and Social Welfare. Toni, or *Sur* (Mr., from *sinjur,* gentleman) *Damato,* as he must be called in his office, is a past president and secretary of the club. He resigned recently as vice-president after a dispute with the committee. At present he holds no office in the club. Nonetheless, he is still called on to lend prestige to it, usually in the form of flowery speeches, at which he is very good. The president of the club is the village baker. Though he derives fairly high prestige from his occupation and his wealth, for he owns a good bit of property, he is not a very imposing figure, and is almost inarticulate. His election to office was a compromise between the Labour and the Church factions in the club. In contrast, the president of the rival Saint Rocco band club, Pawlu Azzopardi, the brother of Victor, the teacher, is an imposing figure and a fine orator. Although he has lived in another town for over thirty years, his high prestige as a teacher, his ability, and his personal qualities have assured him the presidency of the club for almost twenty years. High office in one of the associations may both reflect and confer prestige.

Office in the village branch of one of the political parties may also confer a measure of prestige. The secretary of the local committee of the party elected to form the government has access to power. Requests to government departments and officials often flow through him. He controls important channels of communication. This gives him power. However, prestige does not flow automatically from this. It is easy, in fact, to lose prestige by misusing the power and appearing to exploit fellow villagers for personal gain. However, if he uses his strategic position skilfully, he can usually obtain more prestigeful occupations for himself and his children. Unfortunately, at the time I lived in Farrug, during 1960 and 1961, elected government had been suspended since 1958. I thus had to rely on the tales informants told me of how local party officials acted. In 1960 the only party in the village with a well-organized local committee was the Malta Labour Party. The president and secretary, both skilled industrial laborers, were relatively new to their posts. They had not occupied them before the Labour government resigned in 1958. At the time, of course, they had no access to the government administrative departments. Their positions, nonetheless, gave them prestige among the Labour supporters within the village (approximately 70 percent of the village). However, they were looked upon as the devil's servants by those opposed to the policies of the Labour party. In their eyes office in the Labour Party decreased prestige.

In Farrug a person must behave as a moral person in order to maintain his social standing, his position on the prestige ladder. That is, he must respect the norms of conduct for his various roles. He must be a good son, father, husband, and neighbor. He must also behave as a good Christian. He should be reasonably devout: He should attend church at least once a week on Sunday, and perform all his obligations (women are expected to go to church more often). He should also respect the Church and give it financial support when asked to. The more radical Labour Party supporters, however, make a point now (1961) of not supporting the Church or attending its functions. This gives them prestige among Labour supporters. The opposite is true as far as the rest of the village is concerned.

A man is expected to maintain the moral standing or honor of his family. Honor is difficult to add to, but very easy to lose, for people are expected to behave as moral persons. These moral norms are incorporated in the teaching of the Church and are advocated by the parish priest. They are internalized. They become part of the moral code by which the people of Farrug live. Public failure in some area of the moral code brings with it a loss of honor and, thus, of prestige. There are several families in Farrug (which has, incidentally, and unjustly, the reputation in Malta of being a very tough and rather immoral village) who have run afoul of the moral code and whose prestige has declined in consequence. There have been cases of adultery, theft, embezzlement, wife beating, malicious gossip, assault, and even murder. When these became public, the honor of the individuals and families concerned (each family is a moral community with a collective honor) became blemished. They thus lost prestige even though some scored quite high on other sources of prestige.

In general, the culture of the city has high prestige and that of the country low. Thus, to dress, speak, and behave the way persons from the city do is regarded as more developed and more civilized. The people of Farrug are in constant contact with the towns through work, shopping expeditions, and the radio relay and television. They are conscious of the differences between themselves and town dwellers, especially those who live in Sliema. New styles and customs introduced to Malta through Valletta and Sliema after a time find their way to the villages. When the people of Farrug go into the city, they put on their best (city-style) clothes and accents, but all too often the rough cut and slightly outdated style of their clothes, their sunburned faces, and their rough hands set them apart physically from the more sophisticated townsmen. The same is true of their speech. The dialect of Hal-Farrug is very strong. Most of the younger Farrugin and some of the older ones, with little education but a good ear for accents, have learned to speak *bil-pulit,* as the Maltese equivalent of the king's English is called, but they are not always successful.

Besides language and clothing, certain objects also symbolize town culture and Farrugin strive to acquire them. These include automobiles, television sets, electric refrigerators, gas cookers, and front rooms full of gleaming furniture.[1] The purely symbolic function of some of these objects was apparent in a number of the houses I visited. There, I noticed refrigerators with plastic covers over them. They were used only during important ceremonies such as the annual festa, when the house is thrown open to the gaze of the public. Then the covers are removed and the cooker and refrigerator are moved into the front room or hallway so that passersby can admire them. As far as I know, we were the first persons in the village to use a gas cooker. The following year a number of persons purchased cookers. Some

---

[1] By the summer of 1967 the Hollywood-type bathroom with built-in bathtub, bidet, and enormous mirrors had joined these.

were used purely for show, for the new owners continued to cook on their little kerosene primuses and to take dishes for roasting and baking to the village baker. In one house the cooker had a vase of plastic flowers on it, and in the oven there was a large bowl of oranges, which could be observed through a window in the door with the help of the oven light. However, it is not taking long for Farrugin to learn the more practical uses to which these newly acquired appliances can be put. Many examined them for the first time on television or in the popular ladies magazines (often brought home by daughters employed as maids in Sliema); the same mass media are also instructing them in their use.

Villagers who wish to be considered as having urban manners must also behave in ways which are associated with the town dweller. Going to a shop or bar and drinking wine is considered to be characteristic of the "villager." The stereotype townsman does not do this. Thus, almost without exception the white-collar workers and teachers, whether married or single, rarely set foot in the village's many clubs and the five grocery shops that also sell wine.

Villages, even those as small as Farrug, are also divided into residential areas which have different prestige. The center has the highest prestige, the periphery, in general, the lowest. Thus, the village's best families tend to live near the center on the main street, on the two squares or near the churches. There, they come in contact with each other.

A well-educated person should not eat in public. This also is considered to be a typical village—therefore, "low"—trait. Neither should a person of standing be seen carrying tools or groceries, unless they are very thoroughly wrapped and their contents disguised. This was brought home to me when I bought half-a-dozen 10-inch spikes in a shop that was a few steps from where we were living. As I was returning home immediately, I was going to carry them unwrapped in my hand. Several friends said that this was not nice. I should wrap them. They insisted this was the way that a person of my social standing should behave.

These examples can be multiplied. I have given only a few to show some of the ways in which prestige is derived from and maintained by symbolic objects and behavior which are associated with the more sophisticated urban way of life.

Descent is another factor which can give prestige. This has been hinted at, but not made explicit. The position and relative prestige of a person's parents play an important role in determining his social prestige in the community. The moral reputation, the weaknesses and strengths of one's ancestors, are qualities which, it is believed, can be inherited. Time and again, when people's strong points or, more usually, their moral shortcomings, were pointed out to me, my informants would add, by way of explanation, *Skond iz-zokk, il-fergha,* "Like father, like son" (literally, "As the trunk, so the branch"). By this I do not mean that there are hereditary elite positions within the community.

The relative importance of the factors which affect prestige may vary considerably during a person's lifetime. It is possible to rise to a position of high social prestige: Pietru Cardona, the son of an illiterate farming couple, is now a teacher and one of the village's most important citizens. It is also possible to lose prestige. Victor Azzopardi's sister-in-law, Mananni, was the daughter of one of the village's best families. During her life she moved from the top of the prestige ladder to the very bottom. This descent was brought about by a flagrant love affair that culminated in separation from her husband.

Considerable movement up and down the prestige ladder is thus possible. Nonetheless, the rung occupied by a person's family during his childhood has an important influence upon his life chances. It is obviously an advantage to be born into one of the local top families. Such a family's greater financial resources and interest in schooling ensure a better than average education. This, in combination with the family's wider range of contacts, ensures a good job later, and, eventually, a good marriage. For this reason the quality that I have here called "descent" must be taken into account as an important factor affecting prestige, but it cannot stand alone any more than the other factors already discussed. The example of what happened to Mannani makes this self-evident. The relative social standing of a person in the village is the sum total of a large number of factors. The most important of these have now been summarized.

Patterns of Interaction

Persons in Farrug maintain a pattern of interaction with other villagers which reflects their relative prestige ranking. Each person maintains a network of contacts. What we find upon examining these is that persons of similar social prestige are in more frequent contact with each other than they are with persons of higher or lower prestige. This is perhaps not surprising. Much the same has been observed many times over by social scientists studying the behavior patterns of social classes. The interesting fact here is, of course, that Farrug is what might be called a "one-class community." This interaction between more-or-less social equals is reflected both in the marriages they contract and in the type of contacts they maintain with other persons resident in the village.

Marriage in Farrug, as already noted, is still very much an arrangement entered into by two families who, thereafter, are bound together by certain contractual, religious, moral, and economic obligations. It is, therefore, not surprising that marriages should be concluded between persons who regard each other as social equals. A fairly close examination of the many marriages concluded in Farrug revealed to me that this was, indeed, the case. The wealthier families with high prestige tend to marry among their kind. The same is true of poorer families which occupy the lower rungs of the prestige ladder. At both ends of the scale those who cannot find suitable partners within the village marry outside it.

The operation of these principles can be seen in the pattern of marriages between the village's leading families around 1930. One of these was the family of Angelo Azzopardi, for many years the head teacher of the village school. He came from Zejtun and was posted to Farrug just before the turn of the century as the village's first teacher. His wife, Maddalena, was a sister of the head of the other important family, Lorenzo Brincat, the sergeant of police, mentioned previously. These two families, together with the son of Martin Farrugia, the master builder who remodeled the facade of the parish church, formed the local elite. Their children, with but few exceptions, married well, for they married each other. This is made clearer in the figure on page 52.

Pawlu, the oldest son of Angelo Azzopardi, became a teacher and married in Zejtun, his father's village, where he later became headmaster of the primary school. He has continued to play an active part in the affairs of Farrug as president of the Saint Rocco band club. Victor, Angelo's second son, also became a teacher and remained in Farrug. He married his first cousin, Guza, the daughter of Lorenzo Brincat, his mother's brother. Their children have all received a secondary education, and those who are working are employed in white-collar occupations. Victor has for many years been the village's leading citizen. He is the oldest teacher at the primary school, and was the government-appointed village protection officer during the war. This was a position from which he exercised considerable power. He is also the parish sacristan, the church organist, and director of the village choir. In short, he has been the principal assistant of the village's many parish priests. Angelo's daughter Maria also married her first cousin, Lorenzo's son Nardu. Nardu also had several years of secondary education and became a supervisor with the Medical and Health Department. Those of their children who are working are employed as clerks with the government. Lorenzo's son Alfonso married Angela, the granddaughter of Martin Farrugia, the master builder who remodeled the church's facade. Their children have also prospered, but as their parents died when they were young, they were brought up by their mother's unmarried sister, a government clerk, who saw to it that they were well educated and married well. Another of Lorenzo's daughters, Rita, married a man from Luqa, a butcher at the government abattoir in Marsa, who moved to the village after his marriage. One of their sons married the oldest daughter of Lorenzo's son Alfonso.

The only one of Lorenzo's children who did not marry well was Mananni. Mananni, who died while we lived in the village, was a headstrong girl who married Toni against her father's wishes. Toni was a wild character, a rolling stone with no fixed occupation whose principal interest was heavy gambling, which also landed him in prison. While he was there, his wife committed adultery openly with his younger brother, a handsome lad who later died of a skin cancer—brought about, according to the village, because he had sinned. Toni and Mananni separated. Mananni's family ceased to speak to her. She lost contact with her brothers and sisters. Most of the children of Mananni and Toni are situated near the bottom of the prestige ladder. There is no contact between them and the children of their mother's brothers and sisters.

It is interesting to note that except for Mananni's children, descendants of Angelo Azzopardi and Lorenzo Brincat are still among the village's leading families. The history of these two families is an example of the way in which descent influences the life chances and prospects of persons. It also illustrates the way marriages are contracted between persons of similar social and economic background.

If persons with similar social backgrounds marry, it follows that a person's close relatives, with certain exceptions—such as the case of Toni and Mannani—also have similar social backgrounds. Thus, the network of close relatives with whom a person maintains contact tend to be persons of more-or-less equal social

GUZA
NARDA
NARDU
ALFONSO
ANGELA FARRUGIA
LORENZO BRINCAT
RITA
MANANNI
TONI
MADDALENA
MARIA
VICTOR
ANGELO AZZOPARDI PAWLU

△ MAN   ◭ LEFT VILLAGE   △ MARRIAGE

○ WOMAN

◇ CHILDREN

▲ ● DECEASED

standing. These contacts are particularly important for women, for most of the visiting between women takes place with relatives.

Men have many opportunities to come in contact with other men outside their network of relatives. Their contacts are, thus, not limited to persons of similar social background. Nevertheless, many men spend their free time away from their family in the company of their social equals. The various clubs and wine shops or café's are ranked according to prestige. In general, the clubs have a higher prestige than the wine shops. Of the band clubs, the Saint Martin club, which celebrates the feast of the patron saint of the parish, has the higher prestige. To put it another way, the bar of the Saint Martin club is frequented by persons of a slightly higher social standing than the bar of the Saint Rocco band club. This social distinction between the two clubs is not one that Farrugin themselves make, although, after reflection, they admit it exists. In general, the members of the Saint Martin band club come from families which occupy places higher than their rivals on the village's prestige ladder.

The detailed reasons for this would take us rather far afield at this time. They will be treated more fully in Chapter 6. Briefly, the band clubs came into existence about a hundred years ago as a result of a factional split between those with high prestige and influence in parish affairs and those with little or none. Most of Malta's villages and towns contain band clubs, social clubs, or political party clubs which reflect similar cleavages.

The football club, a relatively new club, was established in 1954. It has become neutral ground on which the partisans of Saint Rocco and Saint Martin can meet. It has a slightly higher tone than the more traditional band clubs. For this reason Pietru Cardona, the schoolteacher, and the sons of Victor Azzopardi, the sacristan, sometimes go there. Although these young men are ardent supporters of Saint Martin, they go into their club only on special occasions such as committee meetings and, of course, for the annual feast.

There are a large number of persons, for the most part married men, who never go into the wine shops or the clubs. Some, such as old Victor Azzopardi, though an active committee member, regard the club bar and wine shops as too common. They wish to maintain a certain amount of social distance between themselves and the rest of the village. They are, after all, members of the local elite. Others are men who have married into the village. They do not go into the clubs much either. They still feel themselves outsiders. The band clubs belong to the Farrugin. Tereza Abela's son-in-law Leonard said he could not afford to participate in club affairs. Another reason, however, is that after ten years in the village he is still looked upon as an outsider. He devotes his free time to his family and to his part-time business of buying and selling poultry and eggs. In general, however, married men do have less free time to spend in the clubs and wine shops than do unmarried men.

There are also noticeable differences in the network of contacts outside the village that persons from different levels in the village's socioeconomic hierarchy maintain. In general, persons who have higher social status within the village have a wider network of contacts outside it. This wider network, in its turn, contributes to the prestige and influence of the person. Their contacts outside the village derive partly from friendships made during their secondary-school career, but they also include many persons met in the course of their employment. Finally, their greater degree of sophistication and knowledge of urban manners allows them greater freedom of action once outside the village.

The principles that I have been discussing are brought out clearly by the behavior of Pietru Cardona and Salvu Vella, who have similar social backgrounds. Both are about thirty years' old now. As children, they used to play together, for they lived opposite one another. Now, they see very little of each other, though they both are unmarried, still live at home, and work in Farrug. Pietru belongs to the village elite, and Salvu is part of the large mass of persons clustered around the middle of the local prestige ladder. If we examine their backgrounds more closely, using as variables the sources of prestige discussed earlier in this chapter, the reason for this difference becomes clearer. To begin with Pietru has had a much better education. Though Pietru's mother is a widow with a very limited income derived from farming, she managed to send her son to a private secondary school. He also attended the teachers' training college. Salvu's father, an extremely intelligent, well-to-do farmer who is the public weigher in the village, also sent his son to secondary school, but Salvu showed little interest in school, and after a few years dropped out. Pietru's education made possible his present employment as one of the four teachers in the village. This gives him great prestige. Salvu's occupation is at the other end of the prestige continuum. He takes care of a herd of fifteen milk cows and cultivates some of his father's fields. He works under the authority of his father who, though he no longer works, still holds the reins of the family enterprise firmly in hand.

Salvu's father is considerably better off than Pietru's mother, but Pietru, with his regular cash income, supplemented by the proceeds from the crops he cultivates with his mother, is, personally, considerably wealthier than Salvu. In fact, the latter often indicated to me that his father kept him rather short of pocket money. As an active young unmarried teacher, Pietru has been asked to play a responsible role in village and parish affairs. While we lived in the village, he took over old Victor Azzopardi's offices as treasurer of the Saint Martin band club and procurator (administrator) of the confraternity of the Blessed Sacrament. He is also president of the boys' section of Catholic Action. Moreover, he helps the parish priest organize fund-raising fairs and other church activities such as pilgrimages and outings to Church rallies against the Malta Labour Party. Salvu, however, has much less free time. His cows take a great deal of looking after both day and night. Though a member of the confraternity of Saint Rocco and the Saint Rocco band club, he holds no office in any of the parish associations, nor does he take any part in their activities. Pietru belongs to the leadership element of Farrug; Salvu does not.

There is also a noticeable difference between the two men in their degree of sophistication. Pietru's speech has less of the village dialect in it. Except when he is working in the fields, he is usually dressed in shirt, trousers, and shoes. When he is in school, he usually wears a tie and jacket. I have never seen Salvu in either tie or jacket. In fact, in the summer he is usually dressed only in a pair of shorts and an undershirt. The only time I saw him wearing sandals, trousers, and a sport shirt was during the village feast. The Farrug dialect is also much more evident in his speech, though he has a keen ear for language and has learned a good bit of English.

There is also a noticeable difference in their circle of contacts. As they are unrelated, they do not meet as kinsmen. Pietru does not go to the wine shops and only very rarely stops by the bar in the Saint Martin club or the football club. Salvu's behavior contrasts with Pietru's. He very often stops in for a pint or two of wine in the little café located near their houses, run by Pietru's aunt. Moreover, he calls regularly at the bar of the Saint Rocco band club. However, he never goes near the football club and never joins the circle of the village notables who spend much of their time chatting with the parish priest on the latter's doorstep. The only contact they had was through me, for I regard both as friends.

It is quite obvious then that though they once played together and they live very near each other, Pietru and Salvu belong to interactional networks that do not interconnect. They do not meet. This is consistent with the noticeable differences in the positions they occupy in the socioeconomic hierarchy. Although they have certain common characteristics, Pietru has acquired attributes which give him more social prestige. These are his education, his occupation, the offices he holds, his urban sophistication, and the symbolic behavior and wide range of contacts outside the village he has through school friends, occupation, and participation in various Catholic associations.

Pietru has been able to make a better adaption to the changing conditions in Malta. His family has not only maintained its position in the village prestige system; it has, in fact, been able to climb higher. Salvu's case is just the opposite. His father was very well educated for his time. As secretary of the Saint Rocco band club and procurator of the confraternity of Saint Rocco, he was for many years one of the village's most important citizens. Salvu has none of these attributes. His social standing in the village, relatively speaking, is much lower than his father's, and decidedly inferior to Pietru's. In terms of the socioeconomic hierarchy of the village, Pietru has moved up, while Salvu has descended, and with them their respective families. This movement up and down must be seen primarily in terms of the village prestige structure. High standing in Farrug does not automatically mean high standing in Malta as a whole. Other prestige systems operate in larger villages, and yet others for the island as a whole. The prestige of those who live in Farrug, measured against these, is relatively insignificant.

The prestige system that has been examined in some detail here is, thus, really typical only for the village of Farrug. This is a subject to which we shall return in the final chapter.

5

Religion and Social Form

THE PEOPLE OF FARRUG are extremely devout Roman Catholics, as are most Maltese. The origins of the Catholic Church in the islands and its economic and political influence were touched upon in Chapter 1. The importance that religion occupies in its many aspects, as a system of both belief and action, strikes all visitors to Malta forcefully.

The following two chapters indicate some of the ways in which religion is enmeshed in the lives of the people of Farrug, both as individuals and as members of groups. Religion orders the rhythm of their lives and provides the structural form of the community in which they live. Participation in its ritual engages them intensely. These rituals, in turn, reflect and provide many of the organizational principles of their society. Their religious belief also has a marked effect on the things they do and do not do. It defines and enforces the moral limits of their behavior. It also influences their relations with fellow villagers and, above all, with persons outside Farrug whose decisions affect their lives. The increasing rhythm of industrialization and the contact the people of Farrug have with the world outside is modifying the traditional role of religion.

Religion and Social Time

Most of the people of Farrug regulate their lives by the periodic religious activities. The major divisions of the day are rung from the bells of the parish church. They first ring the Paternoster at 4:00 A.M., half an hour before the first Mass. Then they ring again to announce the first Mass and the subsequent Mass. Other bells indicate to those outside the church the important stages of the Mass. The peal of the individual bells is known to all in Farrug, as are their names, for each is blessed and christened. The Angelus bell then rings a call to prayer at eight in the morning, again at noon and at sunset, when the Ave Maria is rung to mark the end of the working day. The final bell of the day, *Tal-Imwiet* ("of the dead") is rung two or three hours after sunset. It sounds a brief request to the living to remember the dead in their prayers. The call of the Angelus is observed by many in Farrug. When it is rung, work and conversation stop briefly, and many of the older men remove their hats. Some people—mostly, devout girls and older men and women—also kneel in the street when the bells announce the elevation of the Host during a sung Mass and during Benediction in the evening, but their numbers are dwindling. Finally, late in the evening, small clusters of close relatives gather in their houses, their courtyards, or in their open doorways to recite the rosary together before they go to bed.

Most girls and women and many boys and men attend one of the two Masses offered daily in the parish church. Virtually everyone goes to one of the five Masses offered on Sundays. The few who do not attend are well known to the village and to the parish priest. They are the subject of gossip and a good deal of other social pressure. Since the recent dispute between the Malta Labour Party and the Church, however, their numbers have increased, and the social pressures brought to bear upon them have become noticeably less effective.[1]

Friday is also an important day. It is the day on which Christ was crucified. In memory of this the people of Farrug, and many Catholics the world over, do not eat meat on this day. Many also do not eat meat on Wednesday. It is believed that the Virgin Mary proclaimed that those who wore the Carmelite scapular and abstained from eating meat on Wednesdays would be freed from Purgatory on the Saturday after dying. The cult of Our Lady of Mount Carmel has many devotees in Farrug, and in most of the southern villages. They do not eat meat on Wednesdays, and they wear two strips of cloth, hanging down breast and back, which symbolize the scapular.

The first Friday of the month is honored by special devotions. Outside priests come to the village to hear confessions, and a special Mass is held for school children. This is done to solemnize the devotion to the Sacred Heart of Jesus. The third Sunday of each month is also important, for the Eucharist in the parish church is then renewed and dedicated. After the seven o'clock Mass the Confraternity of the Blessed Sacrament escorts the parish priest carrying the Eucharist through the principal streets of the village. The small procession is usually led by Pietru Cardona, carrying the confraternity's big standard.

As the church bells mark the important hours of the day, so the principal divisions of the year are emphasized by special parish feasts and processions. Besides being major religious occasions, they are eagerly looked forward to as recreational events. Though secular spectacles such as political rallies, the government-run carnival procession, and, above all, cinema and television are becoming increasingly important, the principal amusements of the Maltese still generally have some connection with their religious ceremonies. Each new religious year begins with Easter and ends on Good Friday. The feast of Saint Joseph the Worker is celebrated on the first of May with a short procession in the square in front of the church. Ascension day is celebrated forty days after Easter. At the end of May there is a

---

[1] A number who ostentatiously boycotted church services during the political crisis in the early 1960s were, in 1967, again attending Mass regularly, but many have remained away.

short procession with the statue of Our Lady of Fatima carried by the men. Most of the people escort her through the village. In June Corpus Christi is celebrated. The parish priest, carrying the Eucharist, is escorted by the Confraternity of the Blessed Sacrament and passes through the principal streets of the village. The houses are decorated especially for the occasion and red damask tapestries hang from the windows.

June is also the month of the feast of Saint John and the feast of Saint Peter and Saint Paul, *L-Imnarja*. On this feast there is no procession in Farrug. Many families proceed to the Buskett, Malta's only wood, where they spend most of the night before the feast eating fried rabbit, drinking wine, and singing. On the feast day they rise to see the agricultural show in the Buskett, the religious procession in Mdina, the Island's ancient capital, and to watch the bareback horse races that take place just outside Rabat. These festivities are a very old tradition among the rural population. In fact, some women used to write into their marriage contracts a clause obliging their husbands to take them to Buskett on *L-Imnarja*. Because of its rural tradition it has been regarded as a common affair by the urban upper classes, but recently tourists and foreign residents have also begun to show an interest in the *L-Imnarja* celebration. This is making *L-Imnarja* legitimate entertainment for the status conscious middle and upper classes, who are always quick to reflect the interests and tastes of visiting foreigners.

Throughout summer the feasts of titular saints celebrated in surrounding villages attract hordes of Farrugin. Every weekend there is at least one festa, but on Santa Marija, the feast of the ascension of Mary on the fifteenth of August, there are no less than nine (seven in Malta, and two in Gozo). A number of persons from the village make a point of visiting all seven in the course of the day. Santa Marija is an important day to farmers as well. It follows the harvest and marks the beginning of another agricultural year. It is a tradition to pay land rents on this day.

The biggest feast of the year is the celebration of the feast of Saint Martin, the village's patron, which falls on the first Sunday of September. As will be seen in the following section, this is a very special day in the village. A few weeks later the feast of the Holy Rosary is celebrated and the end of October and the beginning of November the villagers celebrate All Saints' Day and All Souls' Day. They take part in a special procession to the village cemetery. Many also make trips to the big Addolorata cemetery between Tarxien and Marsa. They remember the dead by special services, offering flowers, and caring for their graves.

Later in the month the feast of Saint Martin is again celebrated, this time on his proper day. The patronal feast should be celebrated in November, but the weather then is variable. The festa was sometimes rained out, and many costly decorations spoiled. In 1958 a new festa-conscious parish priest changed the main celebration to September to ensure that there would always be good weather for the feast.

Christmas is celebrated quietly with great devotion. Most houses arrange a nativity scene or sometimes merely a crib in a lighted window. The parish priest gives a prize to the best one. Presents are given—as all over Malta—on the first of the year. This is the day when adults give a traditional present of money, *L-Istrina*, to children. All day children traverse the village rattling their little tin money boxes hopefully. The amounts given range from a few pence to a shilling or two. These gifts are very carefully thought out and remembered. They depend upon degree of kinship, friendship, and upon what a person's own sons and daughters received the previous year from the parents of the children.

Carnival falls on the three days preceding Lent, the forty days of fasting and religious preparation before Easter. It is a traditional time for feasting and general merrymaking. Carnival was once celebrated in Farrug with great enthusiasm. White-shrouded figures used to tell rude stories and sing pointed songs in public about each other. It was a time when moral shortcomings and scandals, kept hidden until then, were made public. However, this spontaneous form of social control no longer takes place in Farrug. Today, the police do not allow people to walk about in carnival disguises, or insult each other with songs. In the past, carnival was often an excuse for a good deal of unpleasantness. It still takes place, however, in a number of Gozitan villages, for in Gozo police rule is generally more personal than in Malta. Today, Farrugin go to see the big government-sponsored carnival in Valletta, with a parade of decorated floats and costumed marchers. In the evenings during carnival week some of the young men of the village go dancing in various hotels, movie theaters, and dance halls in the urban area.

The end of the religious year is signaled by devotional services and processions concentrated into the few weeks before Easter. The cycle starts with Passion Sunday, a fortnight before Easter. The sacred pictures in the church are then draped in black damask. On the feast of Our Lady of Sorrows on the Friday before Palm Sunday, virtually all the inhabitants escort her statue through the principal streets of the village. It is followed by the Palm Sunday procession around the church square. On Maundy Thursday there is a long service during which the parish priest washes the feet of twelve village laymen. An enormous wooden rattle replaces the church bells as a sign of mourning. On Maundy Thursday and on Good Friday in the morning family groups visit the church and pray before the elaborate Altar of Repose constructed in one of the chapels. Many families also make pilgrimages to the thirteen parishes which hold elaborate Good Friday processions. At each they offer prayers before the Sepulcher and pause to examine the statues and funereal hangings in the church before going on. At about two in the afternoon on Good Friday there is a three-hour sermon on the Passion by a guest orator. Many families again leave the village to see the Good Friday procession in one of the villages where such spectacles are organized. The processions are impressive devotional exercises in most villages, but in a few, such as Hal-Qormi, the devotional aspect is partly forgotten in the blaze of publicity and the mass of outside spectators and sweetmeat vendors that accompanies the procession. The Good Friday processions include a large number of heavy statues depicting important scenes from the life of Christ. Many of those who carry the statues have protected their right to do so by notarial acts. They are escorted by scores of persons dressed as Roman soldiers and Jews. Many masked penitents walk barefooted or crawl the length of the route dragging heavy chains or carrying enormous crosses. It is a most solemn and impressive spectacle.

Just after midnight on Easter morning church bells ring out joyously with the announcement of Christ's resurrection. In Farrug, old Victor Azzopardi, the sacristan, and his son remove the black damask signs of mourning from the church walls and sacred pictures. The new religious year has begun.

Religion and Structural Form

As religion provides the rhythm and orders the flow of time, so the Church orders the social space around the parishioners of Farrug. The Catholic Church is a hierarchical organization. The Maltese islands form a single province of the Catholic Church. This province is divided into the archdiocese of Malta and the diocese of Gozo, which includes the small island of Comino. The bishop of Gozo is suffragan to the archbishop of Malta. That is, he is subordinant to the archbishop in certain matters, the most important of which is that the archbishop's court functions as a court of appeal for cases heard in the court of the bishop of Gozo.

The archdiocese of Malta is divided into fifty-three parishes. Every village in Malta and Gozo is a separate parish, though some towns are divided into two or more parishes. The parish is the basic social and territorial unit of the Church. Its limits are fixed by the bishop. In the case of Farrug, they extend little more than a quarter to half a mile beyond the built-up area of the village proper. Each of the parishes and the many Church associations that are tied to them, are ranked. Each has its fixed position in an over-all order. Position and hierarchy are determined by seniority of foundation—in the case of parishes and associations—or date of ordination or appointment to present office—in the case of the clergy—in combination with certain marks of honor conferred by ecclesiastical authorities in recognition of merit. Besides rank, these honors often bestow the right to certain external signs. These are usually certain items of clothing or ritual objects, which are much prized. For example, the clergy of a church which has received the title of basilica may carry a huge red and gold umbrella in processions. They are also permitted to carry a bell, to wear gold buckles on their shoes and, on certain occasions, to say Mass facing the congregation. The religious processions and ceremonies in the parish provide occasions on which these symbols of rank are made manifest and displayed to outsiders. There is much competition for these honors.

The bestowal of honors is not, in fact, determined by merit alone. In view of their importance as symbols of excellence, such external signs become counters in the competition between parishes and between parish associations. Their acquisition is, thus, a matter of great concern to the entire community, and often becomes the subject of political action. That is, persons and groups try to influence those who make the decisions in relation to their bestowal. Through their network of personal relations, leading village figures, including the priests, try to influence the bishop and the other Church dignitaries who surround him. They also bargain with these authorities, and if an unfavorable decision is handed down, they may resort to an open show of disrespect to signal their dissatisfaction and so attempt to force him to reconsider their claim. The final decision is thus made in response to a great many pressures. The honor usually goes to the contender who can present the best case and apply the strongest pressure. This is normally the largest and most influential of the groups competing for the honor. Thus, the number and degree of honors bestowed on any group or individual are roughly equivalent to its or his social importance in the community.

Much of the competition between the supporters of Saint Martin and those who favor Saint Rocco in Farrug is over such matters of seniority, precedence, or the ability of the contenders to display devotion to their respective saints.

During 1952 and 1953, for example, there was a dispute over an attempt by the Saint Rocco procession to pass along a new street over which Saint Martin's followers claimed exclusive rights. When an inexperienced new parish priest backed the Saint Rocco claim before the archbishop, he brought violently into the open a dispute over which his predecessor had successfully procrastinated for years. The followers of Saint Martin not only refused to celebrate their feast, but succeeded in frightening the unfortunate priest rather badly by exploding an enormous rocket in the drainpipe under his house. Some Saint Martin partisans gleefully told me that the priest was soon transferred to another parish. Moreover, during his entire last week in Farrug he had felt so unsure of his parishioners that he asked the police to escort him between his house and the church. Relations between the Church and Saint Martin partisans were restored when the archbishop modified the Saint Rocco procession route.

The fact that the village of Farrug is also a separate parish is extremely important for its internal social organization. It is not possible to consider it entirely as a secular community. It is both parish and village. Religion permeates the structure of Maltese society to an extent that makes it quite impossible to classify many institutions as either religious or secular. As a secular community, Farrug has no official leader, it owns no land or other property, and its inhabitants are rarely called upon or choose to work for a common end. At the same time, villagers are conscious of belonging to a distinct social entity which is distinguished from other villages by a collective nickname and a common subculture.

As a congregation and a religious corporation, the village seen as a parish possesses a clearly defined territory and legal personality. It also has an appointed leader in the parish priest. The inhabitants of the village meet regularly for worship, to take part in religious processions, and to carry out other devotional activities. Furthermore, they act together to celebrate the annual festa of the patron saint, who symbolizes the unity of the secular and religious aspects of the community, for he is patron of both village and parish. Finally, the village as a parish owns property. Its most important property is the parish church and its contents. A parish church is more than just a central place of worship; it is the focal point of a great deal of the social life of the village and the repository of its collective wealth. The church itself was built by the efforts of countless generations of Farrugin. Its gilded ceilings and silver altar front, its damask tapestries and embroidered vestments, its precious votive offerings and ornate statues represent a fortune amassed over centuries from the savings and bequests of countless villagers. The parish church is, thus, the embodiment of the history of Farrug. It is a showpiece, perhaps not as magnificent as other churches, but which all, even the most anticlerical labour supporters, point out with considerable pride to strangers.

The villagers feel extremely possessive about their parish church. Although the parish priest is its official custodian, the church itself remains always in the vil-

lage, while the priests come and go. This was not fully realized by a parish priest a number of years ago. He proposed to regild the chancel, and his parisheners welcomed the idea. They contributed over £500 for the task. When the workmen had completed the decoration and the scaffolding had been removed, the people of Farrug found to their horror that the priest had placed his own personal coat of arms high over the chancel. He was the first priest in the history of the parish who had put his coat of arms inside their church; moreover, he had done so without asking their permission, or even discussing the idea with them. There was great indignation, but the coat of arms remained in place. A year later this priest was promoted to a larger parish and left the village. People began to ask the new parish priest to have the coat of arms removed. He quite understandably declined to do so. They also unsuccessfully petitioned the archbishop. One morning, less than two months after the old priest had left, the village was startled by the news that the troublesome coat of arms had been hacked away. In its place gleamed the freshly painted coat of arms of Hal-Farrug. Someone had sneaked into the church at night to perform the difficult task. The village had taken the law into its own hands to right an affront to its sovereignty that the bishop and his delegates had been unwilling to correct. Although some murmured at the rather disrespectful way in which the task had been accomplished, all were pleased that the coat of arms had been changed. The former parish priest, notified about what had happened to his arms, called in police, but the detectives got nowhere. The police still do not know who did it, although everybody in the village does.

The parish priest is the official head of the village seen as parish. He is the chief informal leader of the village seen as a secular community. Dun Frangisk, the present parish priest, has been there for but a short time. In fact, he arrived while we were living in the village. He is a young priest, ordained only two years. Before coming to the village he served in a large suburban parish. He is the son of a cabinetmaker and a native of Birkirkara, a town of 8500. He was very young when he came, and had had no experience of the life, problems, customs, and tensions of people in a small rural parish. Nonetheless, as the official representative of the Church he immediately stepped into an existing role of great importance in the community. He has authority in all religious matters affecting his parishioners. He ministers to their spiritual and often to their personal needs. He alone can celebrate the many rituals which mark the important stages in their lives. These rituals of transition include baptism, confirmation, marriage, extreme unction, and burial. He also controls the many ritual activities of the parish as a whole. These are, of course, the daily services of worship and the ceremonies, processions, and feasts with which all Maltese, but above all, countrymen, regulate their days and mark the divisions of the year. Through his preaching and admonition he defines, interprets, and enforces the moral code of the Church, which has become that of his parishioners.

Besides dependence on the parish priest for religious matters which are vitally important to them, many have traditionally looked to him for help in secular fields. Half a century ago, according to the census of 1901, the parish priest was one

The parish church on an August afternoon.

of five literate persons in his parish. As such, he was frequently asked to read and write letters. Because of his high standing in the village, and his contacts with influential people outside it, his parishioners turned naturally to him for advice. He represented their interest to the outside world. In this capacity he served them as lawyer, banker, and business adviser. He was also the traditional source of charity.

Increasing literacy and the ever widening range of contacts outside the village have somewhat reduced the dependence of Farrugin upon their parish priest. The involvement of the state in social welfare and charity further weakened their dependence upon him. The same is true of the recent clash between the Church and the Malta Labour Party, which has many followers in Farrug. Dependence upon the parish priest has been reduced; it has certainly not been eliminated. He is still called on to divide inheritances, to settle family disputes, to file claims against the government, to intervene with prospective employers, and even to contact the police if they run afoul of the law.

The *kapillan,* the parish priest, is still the village's chief spokesman. Many refer to him as *il-principal tar-rahal,* the head of the village. His position, of course, has been reinforced by the absence of any secular authorities who represent the interests of the village. The parish priest has considerable authority. The legitimate power that he wields in the field of religion is occasionally used to punish disobedience in other institutional fields. His powers range from denying absolution in confession to refusing to write a good-conduct certificate. He also has the power to give rewards for services rendered. Apart from doing favors for people who have helped him, he can appoint them to parish offices which confer prestige and authority and, in some cases, are also financially rewarding. These powers serve to emphasize and reinforce his position as leader in the village.

A parish is also a bureaucratic structure. Its head is the parish priest, who is usually an outsider. Assisting him are often one or more priests, natives of the parish, and resident there. There is also, usually, a small group of nuns who run an infant school and teach the girls catechism. Then there are the parish servants. These include the sacristan and his assistants, the procurators (administrators) of the various chapels and pious foundations, and the leaders of the numerous religious associations. These persons, together with a few others, who are either particularly devout, or wealthy, but play no overt role in parish administration, form a circle around the parish priest. They derive authority and prestige from powers he delegates to them. They, in turn, buttress his position, from which their own is partly derived. Their children serve as altar boys and help the parish priest in many other ways. In return, they often receive the necessary recommendations to Church-administered private schools. In time they replace their own parents as members of the influential circle of laymen around the parish priest.

The structure of the parish of Farrug greatly resembles this generalized picture. Dun Frangisk is its head. His mother, father, and sister have moved into his residence to take care of him. They divide their time between Farrug and Birkirkara, for Dun Frangisk's younger brother still attends school there. There is also a local priest resident in the village. This is Dun Martin, the son of a wealthy farmer and feed merchant, who is a good bit older than Dun Frangisk. He is one of the four local teachers in the village primary school. As he is a shy person and greatly afraid of being caught up in the rivalry between the band clubs, he does not play an active part in parish affairs. His work in the parish as a priest is confined to saying Mass in the morning. He sometimes assists Dun Frangisk at the evening service and the Sunday High Mass. There is also a small convent of five nuns of the Sacred Heart of Jesus; these nuns run an infant school and teach catechism to the girls.

Old Victor Azzopardi, the teacher, is the church's sacristan, organist, choir director, and chief vestryman. He also serves as butler for the parish priest when the latter gives a reception. He is assisted in some of his work by his sons and a young married man, Martin Farrugia, who is also an enthusiastic partisan of Saint Martin. The parish priest himself is the administrator of the local church and the pious foundations, the administration of which in other, larger parishes is often delegated to laymen or priests, who receive an honorarium for their services.

Victor is an excellent informant on Church ritual and the history of the parish church. He used to remark smilingly that he had trained no less than nine parish priests in the years that he had been serving the parish. For Farrug, like many other small rural parishes divided by band-club rivalry, is a very difficult post, and the remuneration is very meager. A priest usually does not last very long before he begins petitioning the archbishop to transfer him to a more peaceful and wealthier parish. Farrug is, as it was described to me by an official at the archbishop's curia, a stepping-stone parish.

Considering its small size, there are a large number of religious associations in the parish. The oldest are the confraternities. A confraternity is a lay religious society which is dedicated to a particular saint and offers Masses for the souls of dead members. These societies, called *fratellanzi,* are the oldest associations in Malta, and many date back to the Middle Ages. Formerly, certain confraternities in the larger villages and towns acted as trade guilds. Both men and women may enroll as members, but only men may wear the distinctive habit of the confraternity in processions, in which the *fratelli* play an important part. Entrance to a confraternity is by means of a short religious ceremony and the payment of a small fee. This entitles the newly professed member to share in the indulgences, privileges, and spiritual favors which have accrued to the society. A person can belong to more than one confraternity, and many Farrugin do.

There are three confraternities in Farrug. The oldest is dedicated to the Blessed Sacrament. It plays an important part, as we have seen, in several of the parish ceremonies. It has sixty-eight members. Its procurator, or administrator, is old Victor Azzopardi, although he was replaced by Pietru Cardona, the schoolteacher, while we were there. Pietru inherited the distinctive red mantle of the confraternity from his father, who, in turn, got it from his father. He usually carries the confraternity's heavy red-damask standard during processions. This confraternity is very closely allied with the band club of Saint Martin. In fact, Victor is a past-president of the club and Pietru is now its treasurer.

The smallest confraternity is dedicated to the Holy Rosary. It has only thirty-three members. These, under the leadership of the parish priest, who is also the procurator, organize the devotional feast of the Holy Rosary in October. It has second place in the jealously guarded order of precedence. Most of its members support Saint Martin rather than Saint Rocco.

The youngest and largest confraternity, with ninety-two members, is dedicated to Saint Rocco. This confraternity was established in Farrug in 1876. Within ten years the new secondary devotion split the village into two factions, which later crystallized into opposing social clubs, and then into band clubs. The leadership of the confraternity until a few years ago was identical with that of the Saint Rocco band club. Both band club and confraternity organize the feast of their patron, but a few years ago Dun Gorg, Dun Frangisk's predecessor, took the procuratorship of the confraternity away from Pawlu Azzopardi, Victor's brother, who is also president of the Saint Rocco band club. The parish priest felt—and quite rightly—that Pawlu was using his office in the confraternity to push forward the activities of the partisans of Saint Rocco to the detriment of the village's titular feast. In particular, Pawlu said he would prevent the parish from using the confraternity's magnificent silver lanterns during the centenary of Saint Martin in 1960 unless the Saint Rocco club were allowed to participate in the festivities. Dun Gorg knew that if they did participate they would do their best to wreck the big feast of their rivals. He thus stepped in and took over the principal office of the confraternity. However, Pawlu still remains president of the Saint Rocco band club. It is worth noting that he directs this important activity and acts as chief strategist for Saint Rocco partisans from a considerable distance. As already mentioned, he lives in Zejtun, where he also plays an active role in parish affairs.

There are two other active associations for laymen and laywomen besides the confraternities. One is Catholic Action. The Catholic Action in Farrug is divided into three sections: for women, for girls, and for boys. The parish priest is the head of the women's section. The leader of the girls' section is Victor Azzopardi's niece, Nardu Brincat's daughter Narda (see diagram on page 52). Girls and women meet separately twice a week in the little chapel of the Annunciation just off the main street. Pietru Cardona is the president of the boys' section. This is an active group that uses the parish hall on High Street as its headquarters. The boys' Catholic Action is, in fact, a club for teen-agers, and has its own bar and game room. It also organizes theatrical performances. That is, it did so until political conflict split the village and the sons and daughters of Labour Party members were forced to resign from Catholic Action.

There is another very important lay association in the village, the Society of Christian Doctrine, the strictest and one of the oldest of the lay apostolate groups. It is more commonly referred to as *tal-muzew* or MUSEUM.[1] Members live at home and work alongside others, but they may not smoke, attend any kind of public entertainment, cultivate friendships with nonmembers, read secular newspapers, or join other associations. Men are required to cut their hair short, are not allowed to wear neckties, and must wear jackets in public. Female members, until recently, were obliged to wear the traditional Maltese *ghonnella* and many still do. All members are tied by a promise of celibacy. Since they usually enter the society as children, this promise ensures that all are either bachelors or spinsters. In Farrug there is only a male section. Members meet daily in their own premises under the leadership of their superior, who comes from a neighboring town. They hold devotional exercises, conduct study groups for adults, and teach catechism to the village's boys. They also

---

[1] From its Latin motto *Magister Utinam Sequatur Evangelium Universus Mundus.*

take the boys swimming and picnicking during the long, hot summer vacation. During the political conflict they formed the spearhead of the forces which Dun Frangisk mobilized against the Labour supporters. They organized rallies, processions, and special devotional exercises to combat the influence of those whom they regarded as threatening the position of the Church in Malta.

These various persons form a loosely structured but influential clique surrounding the parish priest. Summarizing very briefly, the most important are Dun Martin, priest and schoolteacher; Victor Azzopardi, the sacristan, past procurator of the Confraternity of the Blessed Sacrament, past president of the Saint Martin band club, and respected senior teacher; Petru Cardona, president of the boys' section of the Catholic Action, procurator of the Confraternity of the Blessed Sacrament, treasurer of the Saint Martin band club, and teacher; Martin Farrugia, the young married man who helps Victor Azzopardi with the church; Narda Brincat, Victor Azzopardi's niece, president of the girls' Catholic Action; and the three oldest members of the MUSEUM group. Dun Martin, Victor Azzopardi, Pietru Cardona, the three MUSEUM members, and Narda Brincat are all in the highest socioeconomic group in the village, for they are all either teachers or clerks.

The structure of the parish can be seen as a series of concentric circles. The Church, represented by the parish priest, forms the center. The first circle is composed of the influential persons who surround him and to whom he delegates a certain amount of his authority. Then, there is a circle of members of the religious associations. Another circle contains the rank and file, the parishioners who practice their religion devoutly, but who belong to none of the religious associations. Finally, in the outer circle, and partly outside it, are those who paritipate least actively in the rituals and sacraments of the Church, and those who have actively turned their backs upon them. There is a gradual progression from the religious to the secular as one moves away from the center.

This concentric model of the parish closely resembles the physical layout of the village. At the center of the village we find the main square in front of the parish church. Around the square are the best residential areas where the village notables live. As we have seen, many of these are also members of the parish priest's circle. Those resident at the edge of the village are often, though certainly not always, the least active in the affairs of the parish. This concentric model not only represents the opposition between religious and secular but it also reflects the bureaucratic structure of the parish. This, in turn, is reflected in the residential pattern. This is the traditional model of a Maltese village. Until recently, there were virtually no completely secular institutions in the village. Even the band and football clubs have their chaplains, linking them to the bureaucratic structure of the parish; but the Labour Party has now established a committee in the village. Though this committee has no premises of its own and usually meets in the football club, its members are active. They play an important part in the affairs of the village, and, by opposition, also in those of the parish. This group maintains no formal links with the parish. It cannot be fitted into the concentric model of the village, unless it is placed outside the last circle. This position does not reflect its important structural place in the village. We will speak about this apparent paradox again in a later chapter, for parish and village are no longer the same.

6

Ritual and Belief

RITUAL, that is, patterned, repetitive action in relation to sacred objects or ideas, is an interesting field of study. Most ritual reflects certain important structural principles of the society in which it is performed. This does not give us the right to say that ritual is simply a reflection of that society, or that it exists to place these principles in relief. The important social principles embodied in ritual may, in fact, be rooted in the religion itself. We examined this in the last chapter. The sharp division between the sexes in most fields of social activity in Malta is reflected in ritual, but it is also a structural principle which the Roman Catholic religion, at least the way it is interpreted in Latin countries, enjoins. It is an example of the symbiotic relation between society and religion. This relationship is also apparent in the two rituals which are examined in the following pages: the village festa as a whole, and one particular aspect of this whole, the religious procession on the day of the feast.

Feasts

Of all village feasts, the most important is always that of the patron saint of the parish church. The patron or titular saint of a church is the saint under whose special protection its founders have placed it. The titular of the parish church thus becomes the patron saint and protector of the village. In addition to the more usual religious ceremonies and processions, people express their devotion to their patron with band marches and tremendous displays of fireworks. These celebrations provide the chief public entertainment of the countryside.

The annual festa, however, is more than a superior religious feast and a time of amusement for the village; it is an event upon which village prestige depends. During the feast thousands of people crowd in from every part of the island. All these visitors have definite ideas on how a good festa should be run; nothing they see or hear escapes their critical attention. The decoration of the church, the lighting of the streets, the quantity and firing rhythm of the exploding rockets are compared with those of their own and other feasts. The reputation of the village depends upon their judgment. This is a matter which concerns everyone, and the village draws together to display itself to outsiders in the most favorable light. Before outsiders begin to arrive, however, much has to be done. House fronts are repainted and new clothes are bought or made. The church is illuminated, its interior is hung with red damask, and its treasures are placed on display. Every year the village tries to acquire at least one new work of art for this display. The principal streets and the square are lined with vividly painted papier-mâché statues of prophets and saints, interspersed with urns from which sprout dazzling branches of electric light. Overhead, scores of colorful arches strung from house to house transform the streets into gaily lighted tunnels. The square is usually draped in flags, and all the clubs are dressed in their festal finery, their doors thrown open to the public. Many brass bands are hired and mountains of firework are fused and made ready. All this involves a great deal of organization, time, and money.

In Farrug, of course, there are two major festas during the course of the year, one for the titular patron saint of the village, Saint Martin, and the other for Saint Rocco. As each saint has approximately the same number of followers, the village is divided into opposed groups which compete twice a year over the feasts of their respective saints. The scale of the festa of Saint Rocco, however, was limited by the church in 1934. This was done to prevent this feast in Farrug, and secondary feasts in the many other villages divided in this way, from totally eclipsing the feast of the parishes' official patron saints. For this reason, and for this reason only, the festa of Saint Martin in Farrug is a much more important affair than is that of its local rival. Whether a festa is in honor of Saint Martin or Saint Rocco, however, it has a number of direct consequences on the social organization of the village.

The festa is an occasion on which group values are reaffirmed and strengthened, as individuals and groups express their loyalty to their patron saint and unite to defend and enhance the reputation of their party and village. At the same time, the central position that the Church, and, in particular, the cult of saints, occupies in the social structure is strongly reinforced. The parish church and the patron saint form the hub around which this festive occasion turns.

A festa is also an occasion on which the bonds of kinship are reinforced, for each family opens its doors to its relations, especially to those who live in other villages. Grown sons and daughters return to their parental home, married brothers and sisters meet, nephews and nieces call on uncles and aunts. Younger children learn to recognize more distant relatives whom they might not see at any other time of the year. In this way they become aware of the network of kin relations that stretches out from their home. As already noted, the festa is also a favorite meeting time for courting couples and a traditional occasion on which marriageable boys and girls are introduced to one another.

There are also important economic aspects of a festa. Each family celebrating the feast—in the case of the festa of Saint Martin, this means all his supporters and a good number of the supporters of Saint Rocco (the others boycott the feast!)— buy and make new clothes. They often buy new furniture and appliances to place on display in their lighted and decorated living rooms. The houses are color washed, and new decorations are made. These involve considerable personal expenses. The heavy consequences of the organizational expense of the feast itself must also be taken into consideration. The feast provides badly needed subsidies to the underpaid clergy who take part in the procession. It also provides supplementary income to many of the bandsmen invited to play. Most are part-time musicians and depend upon this extra source of income to supplement their wages. The same is true for the shopkeepers, café owners, and the nougat venders and mobile canteen owners who stream into the village from outside. All do a thriving business, for the people who throng into the celebrating village are in a gay mood and ready to spend money. Among the wide range of persons who derive economic benefit from the feast, we must not forget the lighting experts who decorate the streets, and those who sell the paper, gunpowder, and other chemicals that go in to the making of fireworks. Feasts, in short, provide tremendous economic activity.

The celebration of the festa of Saint Martin lasts three days and that of Saint Rocco, two days. The festa consists of *religious* ceremonies which take place principally within the church, and *secular* celebrations outside the church. The Maltese themselves make a distinction between these two elements in the festa: They call the former the internal feast, *il-festa ta'gewwa,* and the latter the external feast, *il-festa ta'barra.* These often take place simultaneously. The mixture of sacred and profane which results was brought home vividly to me during the centenary festa of Saint Martin, shortly after our arrival in the village. I was in the church during a particularly solemn moment in the service of worship. Suddenly, there was a nerve-shattering burst of fireworks from the roof of the church. Then, slowly, the sharp smell of burning gunpowder began to drift in through the open doors and mingle with the pungent odor of candles and incense. Incense and gunpowder are ingredients basic to the celebration of a festa. In a certain sense they symbolize the two aspects of the feast, the internal celebration, on the one hand, and the joyous secular feast outside, on the other. In the actual celebration of the feast these two aspects are impossible to separate; as the smoke of incense mixes with that of gunpowder, so religious and secular elements of the feast are also combined.

The actual celebration of the feast of Saint Martin can be divided into three parts: the Triduum or Novena (the three to nine days of spiritual preparation which precede the feast day), the eve of the feast, and the day of the feast. As the feast is usually celebrated on a Sunday so that more people can come, the Triduum days are Wednesday, Thursday, and Friday. High Mass is offered on these days, and in the evenings outside priests are often invited to preach sermons on religious topics related to the life of the patron saint. They are days of preparation during which the elaborate street decorations are hoisted into place. Throughout the days, the village is psychologically conditioned to the festa by salvos of petards, which are often timed to coincide with the ringing of the Paternoster and the Angelus. (The petards are immense and have been known to break windows, for they are frequently made of gelignite that is either stolen or extracted from dud shells and bombs fished up from military target areas by festa enthusiasts.) On the last day of the Triduum, after the final sermon, the village band marches through the main streets. Often the band is preceded by a mass of dancing and shouting enthusiasts of both sexes, waving red scarves (Saint Rocco supporters have blue scarves), silver loving cups, paper umbrellas, lions, and other symbols of their loyalty to their band and their saint. This demonstration often provokes fights between rival supporters. These skirmishes are usually sparked off by the bands of girls who hoarsely shout themselves into a frenzy proclaiming the virtues of their saint and the shortcomings of their rivals. There are no visitors during this part of the feast.

On Saturday, the eve of the feast, there is a High Mass and Te Deum to mark the end of the Triduum. This is followed by a barrage of aerial fireworks. During the day outside priests, brought in specially for the festa, hear confessions in the church. In the late afternoon, visitors begin to arrive to watch the Translation, a ceremony during which the celebrant, usually the bishop, takes a relic of the saint on a short procession outside the church. After the Translation, the various guest bands march through the village and then settle down to play selections from operas and works composed by Maltese bandmasters. The many relatives and friends of the bandsmen join the gaily dressed crowds, which have been streaming in by bus and car or on foot.

For several hours they wander up and down the principal streets, past the nougat vendors, past the dazzling houses with their doors and shutters thrown open to attract the eyes of all to festal drapes and carpets, gleaming cookers, and new refrigerators. The crowd moves on past the packed bars and through the festooned clubs, their silver trophies all on show. Stopping now and then to eat and drink and talk with friends, they move into the church and past the banks of flowers that stand before the statue of the patron saint. From there, now surrounded by the red damask and the cut-glass crowns suspended from the golden ceilings, they pass before the silver altar front and gaze at the jewel-encrusted reliquaries on display beside it. Now and then there is a soft discussion of price and craftsmanship as a new picture or silver candlestick reaches past the guttering candles for the attention of the crowd. Slowly, for many stop to kneel and pray, the people move out through the door and past the bandstand, and on to make the round again.

The climax of the evening comes at eleven o'clock, when the forest of standing fireworks which has been planted in the square is lighted. The second day of the festa closes in a deafening shower of sparks and acrid smoke.

On the morning of the feast day, there is a Solemn High Mass during which some noted clerical orator delivers a lengthy and bombastic panegyric on Saint Martin. Following this, the people retire to their houses for huge luncheons with their close relatives. In the late afternoon the long procession with the statue of Saint Martin moves slowly from the church. The saint, carried by six white-robed *fratelli*, stops on the threshold to take the salute of twenty-one petards and a barrage of smaller rockets, the *kaxxa infernali*, or "infernal box," which lasts up to twenty minutes. As the saint at last leaves the church, he is cheered on his way by groups of shouting girls and women. The crowds are thicker than the night before, and amuse themselves in much the same way. There are also more bands, and sometimes as many as five compete for the attention of the crowd within a few yards of each other.

All the while, the procession, followed by black-clad penitents, solemnly passes through the main streets of the village. Those carrying the saint move with a shuffling step that causes him to bob and turn as though he were dancing. As he passes under balconies, his cheering and clapping admirers shower him with confetti. Then, as the procession nears the church, the final salute of colored rockets is touched off. Saint Martin then enters the church and the Benediction is given. After this the crowd of visitors quickly disperses, as do their cars and buses parked in the roads leading to the village. Soon the Farrugin have their village to themselves again. As the women and girls wheel and pull the children off to bed, Saint Martin men and youths cheer the soot-stained men who made and fired the fireworks. They are the heroes of the hour. They toast one another and the success of their feast. So ends the festa for another year.

A day or so after the feast, Saint Martin partisans organize the *xalata*. This is a daylong triumphal tour of the island in a cortege of hired buses and private cars adorned with pictures and symbols of their saint and club. In every village or town through which they pass they shout slogans and songs in praise of their saint, their club, and the excellence of their feast. Their rivals, of course, stay quietly—often sullenly—at home. Their turn comes later.

The organization of the annual feast requires a long period of planning and preparation. The internal feast is organized by the parish priest, aided by Victor Azzopardi. It is primarily his responsibility to carry out the collections which make it possible. The internal festivities and ceremonies for the centenary of Saint Martin in 1960 cost £302. Dun Gorg, then the parish priest, raised this sum by making three door-to-door collections and organizing two fairs during which donated articles such as new pots and pans, biscuits, and, especially, rabbits were raffled off. The contributors to the parish priest's collections, the donators to the fairs and the many men, women, and children who participated in the fair were almost exclusively partisans of Saint Martin. Dun Gorg told me that he received extremely little for the internal ceremonies from Saint Rocco partisans. The funds he raised were used for the musicians and singers of the sacred music played during the feast, and for the remuneration, transportation, and entertainment of the clerics, including the canons of the collegiate chapter of Birkirkara, who took part in the various religious processions.

The Saint Martin band club organized the external feast. Though Dun Gorg at first was chairman of the committee for the centenary celebrations, he soon realized that all that went on in these confidential meetings was known to the village within a day or so, thanks to the baker's wife. The baker was president of the Saint Martin band club at the time. He apparently told his wife what went on in the meetings. The parish priest is supposed to be neutral with regard to the band-club rivalry, but it appeared that he was favoring Saint Martin supporters against their rivals. The baker's wife used this information to antagonize Saint Rocco women. Dun Gorg found his position increasingly more difficult and, consequently, resigned from the committee. Before he resigned he succeeded in placing young Pietru Cardona on the committee, though at the time the latter was not an officer of the club. Pietru acted as his eyes and ears. After every meeting he reported to Dun Gorg. The two then discussed strategy for the following meeting. One of the problems they faced was that most of the committee were Labour supporters who were not in favor of the traditional firecracker salute to honor the archbishop, who had been invited to officiate. The Labour faction won, but the archbishop, who had learned what was afoot, foiled them by being sick and sending the vicar-general in his stead.

The committee set up separate subcommittees to deal with the important aspects of the feast. These included committees for fireworks, fund raising, decoration, and music. The responsibilities of this committee included hiring the guest bands, and also the conductor and musicians for the all-but-defunct club band, as there were no local musicians left in the village. Toni Damato, the district welfare officer, and the vice-president of the club, took charge of the arrangements for the bands. The production of gunpowder and the noisy fireworks were in the hands of the fiancé of the baker's daughter, a skilled machine cutter in one of the nearby quarries, who resigned to be able to work full-time on their manufacture. Victor Azzopardi, treasurer of the band, assisted by Pietru Cardona, collected funds from the men. Narda Brincat, Victor's niece, assisted by one or two of her friends, did the same for the women. She called on all Saint Martin women every Sunday morning during the entire year preceding the festa to collect a subscription of 2d. per family. Pietru and Victor also organized fund-raising lotteries, fairs, and special appeals, in addition to the weekly contributions of 3d. (and, as the festa approached, 6d.) per family head. They also solicited pledges from leading citizens, who entered their names and the sums pledged on a long list. This method, called *l-arbural,* permits donors to compare their contributions. In addition to the activities of these two, whose collection went to a general fund, each subcommittee also collected funds from members and friends. As the feast neared and the rivalry between the two clubs became more intense, it became progressively easier to raise funds. One evening about two weeks before the feast I was chatting with Tereza Abela and her husband. Suddenly one of her sons ran in to report that Toni Damato and Nardu Brincat were waiting outside. I saw Tereza and her husband exchange glances. Tereza's husband, along with all government industrial laborers, had just received a substantial retroactive pay increase. That was why Toni and Nardu were there. They were trying to raise the extra £30 necessary to hire a band to play on the Friday evening before the feast. They went away with £5 from the Abela family.

Altogether, those responsible for the external feast collected £1163. The fire-

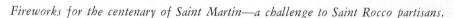

Fireworks for the centenary of Saint Martin—a challenge to Saint Rocco partisans.

works, including most of the gunpowder, were made illegally by the members of the club in their houses, in sheds, and in two abandoned quarries near the village. The cost of their raw materials mounted to around £500. The men and youths spent months converting the raw materials into magnificent fireworks. These, perhaps more than anything else, were responsible for the tremendous success of the feast. Except for extra lighting for the streets and the church, which was done by an outside contractor, all the work involved in decorating the streets was done by the villagers (Saint Martin supporters, of course!). When the feast finally arrived, the organizers were exhausted. The festa itself was an overwhelming success; the greatest festa in the history of the village.

Although the printed program of Saint Martin's centenary carried details of the internal feast and the external feast on separate pages, their celebration took place simultaneously most of the time. The religious procession provided the bridge between the internal and external aspects of the feast, between the incense and the gunpowder.

Processions

Seen analytically the procession is the ritual which links the sacred with the profane. The procession originates in the church, the holy place; it passes out into the secular domain, to the square and the streets of the village; and then it returns once more to the church. Thus, it links the inside with the outside, the religious with the secular. The way in which a religious procession is organized reflects the bridging function which it performs. It is composed of a secular head and a religious tail; the order of precedence is inverted. The laymen, who have the lowest prestige and rank, lead the procession. The celebrant, often the bishop or his delegate, brings up the rear, in the place of honor. Only men and youths take part in the procession; women and children follow it.

With these general principles in mind, let us now look at the colorful religious procession which left the parish church of Hal-Farrug on the Sunday of the centenary festa of Saint Martin in 1960. The procession can be divided into two sections. The first, the secular one, with which the procession begins, was made up of the lay confraternities. The second, the religious portion, was composed of the clergy. The statue of Saint Martin was carried between the two sections, linking the secular and the religious. In the procession, as in actual life, the saint performs the role of intermediary between the secular and the religious, between earth and heaven, between man and God. The standards of the confraternities were carried by members. Their order is determined by their date of foundation with the youngest, of course, leading. The big blue standard of Saint Rocco came first. This was followed by the white standard of the Holy Rosary. The huge red standard of the Blessed Sacrament came last. The statue of Saint Martin followed, carried three abreast by two members of each confraternity. The order in which they are placed around the statue reflects the social position of their respective confraternities and also, incidentally, the position of their respective altars within the church. The order is always the same, and is part of the cultural property of each confraternity. At-

The archbishop, escorted by canons of the cathedral and the Confraternity of the Blessed Sacrament, carrying the reliquary during the Translation.

tempts to change it are vigorously disputed, and can lead to violence. The altar of the Blessed Sacrament is, of course, the central and main altar of the church. Thus, the members of this confraternity occupy the central positions before and after the statue. The two members of the Confraternity of the Holy Rosary walk to the right. Their altar in the parish church is on the right hand or gospel side as one faces the congregation from the main altar. It has the position of second importance. The two members of the Confraternity of Saint Rocco carry the left-hand corners of the statue. Their position on the left here, and the position of their altar on the left side of the church, reflects their junior position.

The statue of Saint Martin was followed by a small bell and an enormous red damask umbrella, the symbols of the Basilica of Birkirkara. The collegiate chapter of that town was invited to add color and solemnity to the celebration. These, in turn, were followed by the cross, which leads the religious portion of a procession. It was carried by a priest and flanked by altar boys carrying silver lanterns.

In many processions a group of altar boys also precede the religious portion of the procession. They also symbolize the link between the secular and the religious, for they are laymen who serve at Mass. The retinue of clergy was made up, as is usual, of a contingent of regular clergy (members of religious orders) dressed in white; seminarians dressed in gold; and, bringing up the rear, the diocesan clergy, with the village's parish priest, dressed in purple.

This group was followed by a huge silver mace, the symbol of Birkirkara's collegiate chapter. Eight canons of the chapter clad in colorful red robes followed the mace and walked just before the celebrant. The celebrant of the procession was the vicar-general of the archdiocese, who was escorted by a number of priests. Three policemen followed the bishop's retinue. Behind them came a group of fifteen women dressed in black. They had taken vows to forego the festivities and follow the procession. The procession left the church at 6:45 P.M. and passed through all the principal streets of the village, returning at 9:30. The exit from the church was marked by the ear-splitting salute of the *kaxxa nfernali*. The return of the saint to the church was signaled by a long display of beautifully worked colored rockets, many of which were made by *Il-Marokk*.

This procession brought into relief and emphasized a number of important structural principles. These may be summarized briefly. First, the central position of the Church in the village was made apparent, for it is the hub around which the procession moved. The hierarchical organizations of the Church was again emphasized by the position of both clergy and laymen. The associations and different grades of clergy were very carefully positioned. These positions are jealously guarded. The passage of the procession from the church through the streets of the village and back into the church also pointed up the concentric form of the parish. In addition to these principles, the procession also highlighted a number of pairs of structural oppositions. These, I have summarized as follows:

Secular	*Religious*
first	last
young	old
outside	inside
left	right
women	men
low prestige	high prestige
weak	powerful
gunpowder	incense

It must now be emphasized that although these dyadic opposites can be distinguished analytically, the people of Farrug do not do so themselves. Participation in rituals is part of their daily life. Processions are as much a part of village life as shopping, gossiping, and going to church. In the lives of the villagers the religious and the secular are not seen as two opposing poles. The way in which these elements are intermingled in the festa itself, as well as in the form and function of the religious procession, is an example of the way in which religious and secular strands are woven into the social fabric of Farrug. The same is true in most of the small-scale, face-to-face societies that are studied by anthropologists.

Besides festas and religious processions, there are, of course, many other examples of the way the sacred and profane are mixed in Malta. For example, priests live at home and not in presbyteries. Most pass the day outside their religious roles, performing secular tasks such as teaching or working in a bank. Images of saints surround one in Malta. They can be seen at street corners, in houses, in offices, and even in Labour clubs. Little shrines and images of personal and collective patron saints are located behind the driver's compartment in all buses. Village and countryside are dotted with hundreds of small chapels. At Eastertime the parish priest blesses the house of each parishioner in good standing with the Church. Secular associations such as football and political clubs are also blessed, and many are dedicated to particular saints. Many Farrugin cross themselves and say a short prayer when they leave their houses in the morning and when they travel in car or bus. These are a few examples to illustrate the degree to which religion permeates the structure of Maltese society. Farrugin move unconsciously from the religious to the secular and back again. They themselves—and this point must be stressed—draw no line between these two social fields. This, I have done, for analytical purposes.

Belief and Behavior

Religion also exercises a very important influence on the value system of the people of Farrug. This, in turn, establishes guidelines and internal models of the way they should behave. The strength of the Church in Malta is derived not only from its strong political and economic position but also from the loyalty of a fervently religious people. It thus exercises an important influence upon their code of ethics. The Ten Commandments and the teachings of prophets and Christ, as interpreted by the Church, have become part of the fundamental beliefs by which the people of Farrug guide their lives. On the whole, they are an extremely moral people who live according to Christian ethical standards. There is little adultery, theft, or violence, and relatively little abuse of power. The little power that is wielded in the village is in the hands of the parish priest himself. This moral behavior is due only partly to the smallness of scale and to the efficiency of the local police, who know a great deal about everyone. It is largely derived, I believe, from the very strong presence of the Church, which defines and enforces this morality. The Christian code of ethics is learned at home at an early age. It is made more explicit and learned by heart during the years of catechism that all children have. It is preached by the clergy and constantly enforced in the confessional and by public opinion. There is a very tight fit between what should be and what is, between the teaching of the Church and the moral code of the people of Farrug.

Another area in which religious belief influences behavior is the political field. I should like to contrast the way in which a person approaches an important decision maker and the way in which he approaches God. A man does not approach God directly. People pray to saints to ask them to intervene on their behalf with God. The saint is closer to God than man is. It is logical, so Farrugin believe, that the saints who once had human form, being in heaven and infinitely closer to God, should intercede on behalf of humans still on earth. For this reason the saints are propitiated. People honor them. Every man, woman, and child in Malta has his or her own particular patron saint, who is his very special protector. In addition to these personal protectors, there are also many other saints to pray to. Saints act as intermediaries between the here-and-now and the hereafter, between man and God, between the supplicant in need of help and the supreme power from whom all help ultimately is derived.

Messages for help are not only transmitted in the religious fields; similar messages are sent in the political field as well. People work through intermediaries. It is believed, especially by the less influential rural folk, that in order to accomplish anything you have to have a protector. That is, you need a patron, someone who can intercede on your behalf with important decision makers. In Farrug the traditional protector and intermediary, as we have seen, is the parish priest. He is the link between the village and the world outside. This role is also played by other important figures: by lawyers, doctors, and wealthy merchants—in short, by persons who are the social equals of the persons from whom they would like to extract favorable decisions. The role of patron is difficult. The services, favors, and protection that he dispenses and the time he spends doing so are limited. They are sought after by many persons. By giving to some he deprives others. In all dealings with government, Farrugin are extremely pessimistic about receiving favorable treatment unless they have an influential protector. They often grumbled to me when they had not been successful, complaining that they had not had the help of a powerful enough *qaddis* or saint. They then quoted the proverb *Minghajr qaddisin ma titlax il-genna,* "You cannot get to heaven without the help of saints."

An example will make this process clear. A Farrug woman whom we shall call Guza wished to secure the special ration of food given by the Department of Welfare to the very poor. She thought she had a good chance because her husband had emigrated, her eighteen-year-old son was unemployed, and she had five daughters of school age to take care of. To get the special allowance, she needed a favorable decision from Toni Damato, the regional welfare officer. She could have approached him directly in the village, for he was readily accessible. She could also have called on him formally in his office in Zurrieq. She did neither. She made an approach to him through the husband of her sister whom she asked, via her sister, to intervene on her behalf with Toni. Her sister's husband was an ardent partisan of Saint Martin and spent a good deal of his time in the club, where he frequently met Toni. Guza knew this. Guza's sister's husband thus agreed to approach Toni on behalf of his sister-in-law. He foresaw few difficulties because he regarded Toni as a friend. He was consequently furious when Toni told him that he could not consider the request. Toni said that he had every reason to believe that the woman's husband was sending money home regularly from Canada. Moreover, he knew that her son, though supposedly unemployed, was actually working in a quarry. Guza's sister's husband, angry at being thus rebuffed, broke relations with Toni. In fact, since that day he has not set foot in the Saint Martin club. He says this is because he is a Malta Labour Party supporter and does not believe in feasts. The interest of this example lies in the appeal that Guza made to an intermediary to help her obtain a favorable decision. She was unsuccessful, for neither her *qaddis* nor her own case were strong enough.

The resemblance between the religious intermediary and the political intermediary is obvious. In a Catholic society, I suggest, the one works as a model for the other. I do not wish to imply that such patronage relations exist only in Catholic societies. This is certainly not so. It is striking, however, that in Catholic societies such relations in the political field are particularly pronounced. The one serves as an example for the other. In the political field people pattern their action upon their behavior in the religious field. The terms of the bargain are similar. The relation between the two forms of patronage is made explicit in the previously quoted proverb.

This chapter has stressed the degree to which religion is an intrinsic part of the various social fields in which the people of Farrug move. Religion is part of their daily life. They make, in their own minds, little separation between the religious field and the secular, between church and state. Religion is not a specialized activity, as it is in some societies. As a priest remarked to me, life in Malta is not like *Time* magazine, where the sections dealing with politics, education, religion, and so on are neatly separated. Nonetheless, there is a pronounced trend toward a compartmentalization of religious activity through its removal from other spheres of social life. This trend is part of the general process of specialization. As Maltese society becomes more complex, social activities become more specialized. This movement toward secularization recently received strong impetus from the clash between the Malta Labour Party and the Church. The Malta Labour Party advocates, as part of its political program, measures which must be seen as a movement toward secularization. It advocates a clear separation between church and state, the institution of civil marriage, divorce, and the abolition of compulsory religious instruction in the schools. It seeks to confine the activities of the Church to the purely religious sphere. These efforts are bringing about a separation between religious and secular activities. This is far from complete. Nonetheless, lines of cleavage between the two can now be distinguished. We saw them in the growing incongruity of parish and village. They have become part of the ideology of a major political party.

To an extent the conflict between the Malta Labour Party and the Church in Malta is itself a product of a more general tendency toward specialization. It can be detected elsewhere as well. I have drawn a parallel between religious and political patronage and pointed to the structural similarity of the intermediary: the saint, on the one hand, and the political patron, on the other. The political patron is interested in doing things for someone else. If his efforts are met with success, the person on whose behalf he intervened will be beholden to him. He can be called on for assistance at some future time. This is the traditional way of handling relations with authority. It is, thus, a mutually beneficial arrangement.

In recent years the Malta Labour Party has built up a powerful political organization. It has a number of paid and voluntary employees, party workers, who perform the intermediary functions of the more traditional patron. That is, they intervene on behalf of party members with higher decision makers. I was assured by many Farrugin that during the period of the Labour government, between 1955 and 1958, they did not need *qaddisin* (saints). They worked through party functionaries who would bring their cases to the attention of the decision makers. Though much of what they said must, of course, be taken with a generous pinch of salt, my informants were contrasting the bureaucratic efficiency of the Malta Labour Party with the traditional patronage based Nationalist Party. There is an important lesson to be learned from what they said. The story points to the replacement of a system of interaction based on mutually advantageous personal relations by a system of impersonal relations based upon cash or bureaucratic duty. The personal relation between patron and client is being replaced by the relatively impersonal specialized relation between paid party employee and party member, who has a right to have his request forwarded through channels to the appropriate authorities.

Some persons also noted that it is no longer necessary to work through intermediaries, whether the traditional patron or the new party bureaucrat. Farrugin are now literate, and increasingly they are well educated. They can, therefore, present their own cases directly to the appropriate decision makers. There is not the same need to become beholden to anyone. To a certain extent I think this development is paralleled by one which is taking place in the religious field. As a result of the second Vatican Council, greater emphasis is being placed upon direct communication between man and God. Religion, henceforth, is to be God centered, and not saint centered as in the past. Communication is to be direct, not filtered via polyvalent middlemen. The multipurpose intermediary is being eliminated. There is increasingly less resemblance between religious patronage and political patronage. This, in turn, is being brought about by the increasing division of labor and the specialization of social relations. These are illustrations of the more general process of secularization which is just beginning to get underway in Farrug.

7

Political Contests

U P TO THIS POINT I have been primarily concerned with presenting the structural form of the village of Hal-Farrug, together with a description of its principal institutions. It is time to take a more dynamic approach. This chapter will be concerned with the ways in which people and groups compete for honor and power. That is, it deals with political competition. Politics, viewed from this angle, is a type of game. There is a certain agreement about the prize, rules relating to who may play and who may not play, and the type of strategy the players use.[1]

The villagers of Farrug are involved in two political games at the same time. The one I have called "parish politics." It is chiefly concerned with the competition between the supporters of Saint Martin and Saint Rocco. The second game I have called "national politics." It involves the people of Farrug in their roles as members of the national electorate. This game involves them in the competition between the Malta Labour Party, on the one hand, and the parties and groups who oppose it, on the other. These two political games are often played simultaneously with the same personnel. The reciprocal influence of the rules and strategies used in one game on the other presents a fascinating analytical problem.

The Maltese call these competing groups *partiti* (singular, *partit*). The term thus corresponds not only to groups of the order which in English we would call "parties" but also to those to which we would apply the term "factions." Political parties are called *partiti;* so are opposing groups which compete over the building of a church or, as in the case of Hal-Farrug, over the celebration of different saints. *Partiti* are said to have *pika* between them. *Pika* denotes relations of competition, ill-feeling, hostility: in short, rivalry. *Partiti* are considered to be a bad thing. They disrupt the harmony of the village and make it more difficult to project the ideal image of village unity to the outside world.

---

[1] The argument presented in the following pages owes a great deal to Bailey's penetrating theoretical analysis of encapsulated political systems (Bailey 1969).

Parish Politics

The oldest permanent division that exists in Hal-Farrug is between the supporters of the two rival band clubs. This division is related to the cult of saints. Hal-Farrug, in common with a large number of other parishes, celebrates two saints: the titular of the parish, Saint Martin, and the secondary saint, Saint Rocco, who has assumed almost equal social importance.

The story of the origin and development of the festa *partiti* in Farrug is in many respects similar to the accounts which I collected about festa *partiti* in other villages. It is helpful, therefore, to examine it in some detail. Before 1877 there were no festa *partiti* in the village; everyone cooperated for the celebration of the feast of Saint Martin, the patron of the parish. By all accounts this festa was a humble one, and lasted only one day. This period is described as an idyllic time, a sort of mythical period during which the village was happy and united. In 1876, however, a new parish priest arrived, and the scene began to change. Dun Rokku, the new priest, not only had a strong personal devotion to the saint after whom he had been named; he was from a village where there was a strong secondary *partit* devoted to Saint Rocco. Within a year he established a confraternity dedicated to Saint Rocco in Farrug in order, according to Pawlu Azzopardi, the actual president of the Saint Rocco's band club, to inject some more life into this rural parish. The first feast in honor of Saint Rocco was celebrated in October 1878; it also marked the establishment of the new confraternity. Although the new secondary feast was at first a simple affair, it and the titular feast grew rapidly during the next few years. In 1880 the new confraternity established an altar in the church dedicated to its patron. By 1886 some persons were beginning to grumble about having to pay for another feast, saying "You collect for your feast, and we'll collect for ours."

In 1888 an incident occurred which changed the course of the rivalry between the supporters of the two saints, which, until then, appears to have been rather mild, as most people celebrated both saints. Dun Rokku, who was the procurator of the parish church, tried to increase the rent on some of the local property it owned. There was an outcry. Some persons went to the bishop to complain. Not only had Dun Rokku been diverting parish funds collected for other purposes to buy new street decorations for the feast of Saint Rocco, they complained, but also he was now raising rents on church property to continue this work. The complaints resulted in an investigation following which the procura of the parish church was taken from Dun Rokku and given to a prominent member of the village who favored Saint Martin. This was an important loss of power and, in this poor living, a serious loss of revenue. The parish priest had lost the round to the local "establishment," which traditionally organized the celebration of Saint Martin. This defeat, not surprisingly, infuriated Dun Rokku. From that day onward, according to the accounts I heard, he threw his full support openly behind the feast of Saint Rocco, and in so doing divided the village into opposing factions.

Some time after this, each *partit* formed its own social club. According to Saint Martin supporters, their club grew out of a pre-existing band club, but that of their rivals was not established until after World War I. They thus consider that they have seniority. Saint Rocco partisans, of course, deny this. They maintain that both clubs came into being when a pre-existing club split, around the turn of the century. Consequently, they have equal seniority. Both clubs claim that the records crucial to the question of seniority were destroyed by enemy action during the last war. There is, thus, (conveniently!) no documentary evidence which can prove or disprove either claim. This makes for deadlock whenever the issue of seniority is raised.

The two *partiti* came into being over a difference of opinion which split the parish into two factions, but the factions had civic associations at the center: the confraternities at first, and later the band clubs. These provided continuity. They gave a permanent core to the factions, and changed them into enduring corporations for which the term "faction," which indicates a temporary conflict group, is not wholly suitable.

As already noted, there is some relation between occupational class and *partit* affiliation. In general, the supporters of the titular saint have more prestigeful occupations than their rivals. The data I gathered in Farrug illustrate this correlation clearly. As shown in Table 5 below, 83 percent of the village's professional and white-collar workers belong to the Saint Martin *partit,* while only 38 percent of those engaged in agriculture do.

TABLE 5

Partit AFFILIATION AND OCCUPATIONAL CLASS IN 1960

| | | Partit *Affiliation* | | |
	Number	Percentage of Labor force	Saint Martin	Saint Rocco
Professional and clerical	12	4	83%	17%
Service and skilled	115	39	55	45
Semiskilled and unskilled	124	42	48	52
Agricultural	45	15	38	62
	296	100		

It is, of course, extremely difficult, if not impossible, to discover the motives which prompted people to choose a particular *partit* almost a century ago. The only clue, I think, lies in the correlation between occupational class and *partit* affiliation. Apart from this class alignment, I found no evidence in Farrug, or any other village so divided, of any pre-existing structural division out of which these festa *partiti* might have developed. As membership is now inherited, it appears that the position which members of the great-grandfather generation occupied in the village class structure in some way influenced their choice of *partit*. There is some evidence for this, although not a great deal, in the genealogies of the present generation. Frequent marriages with outsiders, emigration, and the changing employment structure of the country over the past six decades have blurred this picture considerably. It is probable that the new cult appealed more to those persons who held no office in the older confraternities of the Blessed Sacrament and the Holy Rosary and who performed no official functions in connection with the celebration of the annual festa of Saint Martin. Through the new cult they could gain offices and perform functions which hitherto had been monopolized by the circle of the village notables who had always surrounded the parish priest but whom Dun Rokku had antagonized. Some informants also mentioned that young men were particularly attracted to the new cult. In this we can see the universal resistance of the young to the authority of their elders, for by becoming active in the new cult, they were asserting their independence from the controls of the older generation. Were the secondary *partiti* then a form of protest against the established authority, a sort of "underdog" party? Everything points in this direction. These less privileged persons responded readily to Dun Rokku's efforts to obtain local support in his conflict with the village notables.

Recruitment to a *partit* is today quite straightforward: a person is either born into a *partit,* or he marries into it. Children support the *partit* of their parents, an outsider marrying into the village, generally that of his (or her) spouse. Marriages between members of rival *partiti* are regarded as undesirable. They also tend to be between persons at different levels of the village's socioeconomic ladder. They occasionally take place, but the division of loyalty within the nuclear family which results often leads to quarrels and, occasionally, to temporary separations. There is a favorite Maltese festa story of a wife who refuses to cook for her husband because he belongs to the other *partit.* This is based on fact. I know a quarry owner, a Saint Rocco partisan, who slept in a tool shed in his quarry during the Saint Martin centenary because he quarreled with his wife over her contributions to the rival *partit.* Of the marriages contracted within Farrug, seventy-two percent took place between members of the same *partit.* Children of mixed marriages support the feast of their favorite parent: Boys normally follow their fathers and girls their mothers.

Children begin to express *partit* affiliation when they are between twelve and fourteen years' old. At this age they are old enough to follow the processions and take part in the demonstrations on their own. Fund raisers make demands on them, and they are asked to help decorate the streets. A youngster would jeopardize his social standing with his agemates if he failed to take a firm position with regard to one of the saints. This would remove him from much of the community's social life. Consequently, by the time a village boy has reached fifteen, he has usually selected his *partit,* thus accepting and becoming part of the fabric of *partit* rivalry which will hold him until he dies or leaves the village.

So much for the origin and social composition of the *partiti.* I may just observe here that the festa *partiti* are not based on territorial divisions. Since upward mobility does not involve change of *partit,* but is often accompanied by a change of residence, most residential areas are mixed. Nonetheless, there is a tendency for supporters of Saint Martin to live in the better residential area near the church, and for their rivals to live in the poorer sections more remote from the central square. This is a reflection of the differing occupational class of the members. I observed much the same pattern in other villages divided by festa *partiti.* In Farrug 65 percent of the people living on the main square and the four streets leading into it supported Saint Martin; only 46 percent of those living in other parts of the village did so.

Disputes between the *partiti* concern matters which affect their precedence and ability to display devotion to their saints. The course which such disputes take

Preparing fireworks for the feast of Saint Rocco, after church on Sunday morning.

is highly formalized. They usually begin when the Saint Rocco *partit* petitions the parish priest for a new privilege. It must do this because of the Church regulations designed to reduce the scale of secondary feasts. Saint Martin leaders then try to check their rivals by threatening to cancel their feast if the privilege is granted. At this point the parish priest passes the dispute up to the archbishop for judgment. Both sides then use all the influence they can muster to obtain a decision favorable to them. If the decision is favorable to Saint Martin, the dispute usually ends quickly, for Saint Rocco's partisans cannot threaten to cancel their feast for fear that the Church might suppress it forever. This has occurred in some villages. If the decision is favorable to Saint Rocco and his followers, however, Saint Martin's partisans refuse to hold their feast for a year or so, or until they can wring some concession from the parish priest or the archbishop. After that a new dispute arises over some other issue, and the process starts all over again.

Let us look, however, at some of the major skirmishes during recent years. From 1952 to 1954 there was the trouble over the attempt by Saint Rocco partisans to let their procession pass along a new street. This was described previously. In 1956 the Saint Martin band club threatened to cancel its festa because the Saint Rocco confraternity had been given permission to renew two of the bunches of artificial flowers which stand on the secondary saint's altar. The following year the Saint Rocco band refused to play at the installation ceremony of the new parish priest because the archbishop had denied its confraternity permission to hang a new picture of the saint over his altar. In 1960 the parish priest infuriated Saint Rocco followers when he did not allow the *partit* to participate in the centenary feast for Saint Martin. While we were in the village, a sharp dispute occurred over which band was to have precedence at the installation ceremony for Dun Frangisk. They could not agree, so neither played. At the moment there is another struggle in the offing. The confraternity of Saint Rocco has been petitioning the archbishop for permission to renew the platform on which its saint stands during the feast. Saint Martin supporters are applying counterpressure and have threatened to cancel their feast if permission is granted, as it probably will be, eventually, for the present platform is old and falling to pieces.[1]

The competition between the followers of Saint Rocco and Saint Martin very much resembles a war game. The action between them takes place within a framework bounded by the decrees of the Church, the laws of the state, and the appropriate body of custom. It is, thus, ordered competition for a valued end. The end or prize is some concession or symbol of prestige for the *partit*'s saint. Players who may take part in the game are determined by birth and marriage. Each *partit,* or team, is made up of a core of men the leaders of which are the committee members of the respective band clubs. These are surrounded by a group of supporters consisting of the women and children. Though these take an even more active part than the men do in baiting their rivals in public, they have no official voice in strategy decisions. The strategy consists primarily of a period of maneuver during which the teams build up strength and prepare their cases. This is followed by a formal challenge, the confrontation, when the petition for a new privilege is delivered to the church. The actual encounter between the two teams takes place over an extended period of time. Each team tries to manipulate its network of contacts, to apply pressure, advance arguments, and gather intelligence, in an attempt to counter its rival's moves. If one succeeds, then it scores over its rival, and that match or round is over, but the game itself continues, as it has for the past ninety years. The size of the teams and the intensity of their encounters have been reduced somewhat by the impact of a rival political game which is played outside the village (Boissevain 1965, Chapter 6).

National Politics

The open conflict between the followers of the Malta Labour Party, on the one hand, and of the archbishop, on the other, has divided Malta into two opposing camps. The origins of this conflict need not detain us here (see Boissevain 1965). We are primarily concerned with the consequences of this dispute in the political life of Farrug. This division, which originates at the national level, has cut deeply into the traditional political life of Farrug. Dun Frangisk, the parish priest, is the leader of the persons who support the archbishop. The most enthusiastic partisans among these are Victor Azzopardi, Pietru Cardona, Narda Brincat, and the leaders of the MUSEUM. The rank and file of Catholic Action and MUSEUM also support the archbishop wholeheartedly. The lay leaders of Catholic Action are, for the most

---

[1] During the summer of 1967 I heard that the first round went to Saint Martin. Although the archbishop's fine-arts committee granted permission for a new platform, the design it approved was regarded by Saint Rocco supporters as too simple and unworthy of their patron. They are holding out for a more beautiful model!

part, also officers of the Saint Martin club, as are the other important persons who help the parish priest.

The Labour supporters look to the members of the village Malta Labour Party (MLP) committee for leadership. These are also mostly prominent members of the Saint Martin *partit*. Most are skilled workers and technicians employed with the government or the dockyard. This committee was elected while I was in Farrug; previously, there were no formal officers. Now, the Labour group in Farrug is tightly linked to the national party structure.

In general, the Labour party recruits its support from skilled and unskilled laborers who work outside the village in the dockyard area and in the industrial departments of the government. They are opposed, speaking again in very general terms, by the professional and salaried classes and the farmers, who support the Church. The Labour party secured a good measure of support outside these rough lines during the three years it was in office. It did this by helping the farmers, establishing social assistance and health schemes, building many new schools and other public works, and by officially transferring the hiring of casual government laborers from the hands of patronage conscious politicians to a government labor office.

However, the increasingly anticlerical policy of the Labour party, as well as the heavy sanctions the Church began to impose on it, have alienated many Labour supporters. During 1961 the Church took firm steps to make people choose between it and the Labour party. The archbishop interdicted most of the Labour party leaders. He also instructed confessors to deny absolution to those persons who read, contributed to, printed, or sold the Labour newspapers. Individual priests also refused absolution to those who attended MLP meetings or showed sympathy for it in other ways. They portrayed Dom Mintoff, the Labour party leader, as a socialist devil working to give the islands over to Communism in the manner of Cuba's Castro. These severe measures remained in force until recently.

About seventy percent of Farrug supports the Labour Party, though considerably fewer are dues-paying members. Both festa *partiti* reflect this division. There are, however, relatively few occasions when all the supporters of either the Malta Labour Party or the Church face each other as groups at the village level. The few times I saw this occur were during national rallies. May Day 1961 provided such an occasion. In the morning the Labour supporters, mostly men, went to take part in the big Labour parade in Valletta. The same afternoon their opponents from the village, mostly women and children, went to the archbishop's rally just outside Valletta. While the groups were gathered in the village, there was a good bit of name calling and singing of appropriate songs: the Catholic Action girls sang the papal hymn, and some of the Labour enthusiasts sang their own words to the same melody. During the year there were also a number of incidents in the village which were directly related to this political tension. Slogans appeared on the walls; the parish priest had to tell a young Labour supporter to leave the church for being rude; unknown persons destroyed some decorations of the MUSEUM; and someone set fire to the front door of a shop belonging to one of the Labour leaders.

The game being played out in the national political arena in certain respects resembles the traditional game between the festa *partiti*. To begin with there is a clearly defined prize, namely, victory at the national elections. Each side attempts to increase its personnel at the expense of its rival. The teams competing in the national political arena are also relatively clearly delineated. The personnel who may play formally are those adults old enough to vote. The core of each local team is composed of the village leaders: the parish priest and the influential circle of persons around him, on the one hand, and the committee members of the Malta Labour Party, on the other. Each core group is surrounded by a large number of followers and younger men and women and children. The strategy of the two national political teams differs slightly from that of the festa *partiti*. To begin with it attempts to subvert followers from the other team. Attempts are made by various means to get members of the rival team to cross over. This is an important strategic move. A challenge is made when one party considers itself strong enough to win. The encounter is decided by the electorate. At the national level this takes place during the election, but in the village arena it may take place during the council meetings of the various associations that are divided by factions originating in the national political arena.

The Village Arena

Two different political games are being played out at the same time, in the same local arena, and with the same personnel. This creates a number of grave problems for the people of Farrug. Prizes, rules, and loyalties generated in one political game have an influence on the other game. In looking at the village as a whole, as has been noted, two important principles of organization—loyalty to a certain saint and loyalty to a political ideology—have divided the Farrugin into various opposing groups. Virtually every person in the village is committed to supporting one of the two festa *partiti,* and has taken a position for or against the Labour party. These principles, in turn, form potential lines of cleavage in the formal village associations.

The two band clubs are exclusive units with regard to the festa rivalry. The boy's Catholic Action is, in effect, also an exclusive group, for after the parish priest chased out the sons of Labour supporters, only about eight young men remained. All of these are Saint Martin supporters. Although the MUSEUM members are mixed, their important issues concern spiritual matters. They have successfully divorced their association from the festa activity. The Labour committee is also mixed with regard to festa rivalry, but thus far, this has not been a source of conflict within the group, possibly because the Labour leaders are also important members of the Saint Martin band club. The members of the girl's Catholic Action and the football club include some of the most vocal partisans of Saint Martin and Saint Rocco. This results occasionally in the division of these associations along festa *partit* lines. The football club was almost deserted during the two months preceding the Saint Martin centenary, when rivalry between the festa *partiti* was running very high. Both societies try to avoid division by taking no formal part in the celebration of the two festas.

The situation with regard to political loyalty is somewhat different. The

MLP committee and the Church societies are exclusive groups. In practice the football club is as well, for all its active members are Labour supporters. That leaves only the band clubs with political mixed membership. Open conflict between rival political partisans has not yet occurred in the Saint Rocco club, although the lines of potential cleavage are present. This is chiefly because the leaders of the club have made it a matter of principle to suppress their personal political feelings in order to preserve the unity of the club. They feel that only as long as they are tightly united can they survive as a *partit* in the face of the Church's determination to put an end to festa rivalry by reducing secondary feasts and eliminating the secondary *partiti*.

In contrast, the continued existence of the Saint Martin *partit* is not threatened by the Church. Indeed, the Church's policy is to build up titular festas at the expense of secondary celebrations. It thus does not have the same functional need to remain united, as does its rival. This has made it more vulnerable to internal dissension. Moreover, we have also observed that both the MLP supporters as well as their opponents are led by persons who are at the same time leaders of the Saint Martin club. At club committee meetings these persons continue to oppose each other over many issues of club policy. This division among the club leaders causes the rank and file to take sides. If the dispute is resolved rapidly, it has no effect on the unity of the group; but if the conflict remains unsettled for some time, all members may be asked to align themselves. At this point the continued existence of the club as a united corporate body is seriously threatened by the possibility of one of the groups leaving the club. This physical division is usually avoided by the activity of peacemakers, who place the unity of the club over partisan loyalties. For example, during the recent centenary celebration, the Saint Martin band club was divided over whether to fire the traditional salute of firecrackers for the archbishop when he came to take part in the festa. The Labour element won, but there was bitter feeling over the matter. This, however, disappeared when the archbishop announced that he could not come. The opposing elements in the club then united and celebrated a rousing feast, much to the chagrin of their rivals. In 1930, however, the club actually did split in two over a similar crisis between the supporters of Lord Strickland, on the one hand, and the archbishop, who opposed him, on the other. The two clubs eventually reunited, but not until the political conflict at the national level began to subside following the suspension of the constitution in 1933. When I left Malta in 1961, the Saint Martin club seemed to be facing such a crisis again. The young Labour members had just successfully boycotted the festa of their patron saint in retaliation for the attacks of the Church on their political party. Older members of both political colors, who remembered the bitterness of the 1930 split, were trying to bring the opponents together to avoid an open breach in club unity.[1]

The game of parish politics, as noted, has very little influence upon the national political game. The contrary cannot be said. Some of the conflicts created by this division have been emphasized. There is another aspect which is equally important. This is the slow but sure change which is taking place in the way in which the game of parish politics is being played. This has been brought about by the national

---

[1] Upon my return visit in 1967 I learned that they had succeeded in preventing a split, but not without great difficulty which had cost most of them their offices in the club.

political game. These changes are not merely temporary; they are deep-going. They are structural changes; that is, they are changes in the rules of the game. Very briefly, a growing number of persons from the Labour team are rejecting the prize of the game of parish politics.

The feast of Saint Martin the year following the centenary celebration is an example. The initial reaction of the Labour faction within the Saint Martin club to the attack of the Church on their political party was to boycott the feast. There was also, however, an ideological reason for the boycott which the leaders of the Malta Labour Party had been propagating for years. Namely, such feasts are a waste of money and they reinforce the position of the Church. The policy of the Malta Labour Party is to channel as much energy and funds as possible into the development of the country. It sees the investment of energy and funds in the celebration of feasts as detrimental to this aim. It is, therefore, opposed to such feasts on ideological grounds. These ideas are gradually being accepted by Labour leaders in Farrug. They thus reject the prize, the rules, in fact, the entire game of parish politics. This has brought about a reduction in the persons playing the game. In 1961 the Labour faction of the Saint Martin *partit* boycotted their feast. The rejection by a number of Saint Martin partisans of the festa's game itself has reduced the personnel. This has weakened the Saint Martin *partit*. Although those who remain as active participants in the game tend to work harder to compensate for the loss of many of the most active supporters, their efforts are not quite enough. Some of the intensity has gone out of the game.

All this should not be interpreted as an eclipse of the game of parish politics. This is far from the case. The parish feasts continue. Moreover, they are bigger, more crowded, and noisier than ever. This is primarily because more money is coming into circulation. Consequently, the contributions of fewer people can maintain or even increase the size of the feasts. Transportation is continually improving, thus enabling more relatives, friends, and general festa enthusiasts than ever before to pour into the village. The 1967 festa of Saint Martin, though still boycotted by Labour members of the club who had been among the saint's most active partisans during the 1960 centenary, was a rousing success. In fact, it compared favorably with the centenary for the reasons just enumerated. To these reasons may be added two more, one general to all Malta—for the festas during the summer of 1967 were everywhere bigger than they had been for many years—and the other specific to Farrug. The general reason is the relative abatement of national political rivalry. The bitterness aroused during the 1966 national elections has passed. Most villagers enjoyed being able to spend time, energy, and money on a well-known, popular activity relatively unrelated to national politics. It made a welcome change. Secondly, 1967 was the first year the new Saint Martin fireworks factory came into full production. The workers outdid themselves to show their rivals of what they were now capable; and unquestionably, the colossal colored rockets of the 1967 festa were superior to those of the centenary!

Nonetheless, there has been a change. There are now fewer people actively participating in the game of parish politics. This is the result of the intrusion into the arena of a new game with new prizes, new rules, and a new ideology.

The intrusion of national politics into the traditional arena of parish politics is not the only reason for the reduction in rivalry between the festa *partiti* in Hal-Farrug. In part, it is also a reflection of a more general trend toward secularization. It has been shown how the confraternities provide the corporate centers for the competing groups of saintly partisans. Since the war, however, there has been a steady reduction in the intake of new members into these confraternities. Younger men are simply not joining them. A few young men, such as Pietru Cardona, continue to take an active part, but they are exceptions. The confraternities are slowly dying.

There is also another factor partly responsible for the gradual decrease in festa *partit* rivalry. This is the increase in the number of other leisure associations. The Farrug football club came into being in 1954. Since then it has become the most popular club for young men in the village. It is a place where partisans of both Saint Martin and Saint Rocco, who would normally never set foot in each other's clubs, can meet on neutral ground. The band clubs must now compete for the free time and interest of the young men. Many of the men around twenty years old find the rather oppressive decor and conservative policies of the band clubs, which are still run by the older generation, less exciting than the football club.

Emigration has also dealt a severe blow to the band clubs. During the 1950s about twenty of the most active musicians and fireworks experts left for Australia and Canada. Since their departure neither band club has been able to muster a local contingent of bandsmen. They must rely upon hired outside musicians during the festa. Continually improving transport facilities to the neighboring village of Luqa and to Valletta have placed the cinemas and bright lights there in direct competition with the very limited entertainment of the village. In short, there is an increasing rhythm of contact between Farrug and the rest of the island.

The social horizons of the inhabitants of Farrug are no longer those of the parish. Purely village-based activities are being supplemented and sometimes re-

Members of the Farrug Stars Football Club.

placed by countrywide activities and associations. The intrusion into the parish arena of national politics is but one example of this. This is an index of the steadily increasing tempo of communication between Farrug and the rest of Maltese society. The line between the village section and the national whole is becoming less and less distinct. The encapsulated rural village is being absorbed into the nation. Elements of the former isolation will continue to persist, even as the game of parish politics will continue for many years to engage the attention of large numbers of Farrugin, but the trend toward their greater involvement in the social, economic, and political life of the country as a whole is clear.

8

Village and Country

U P TO THIS POINT Farrug has been examined as a whole. The focus has been on the village and the social relations contained therein. Throughout this study, it has been apparent that there is a growing involvement of the village with the society around it. Farrug is not an isolated whole. It is in contact *with* Maltese society. It is also a part *of* Maltese society. We must now ask more about the nature of the contacts between Farrug and the rest of Maltese society, the relation between a part and the whole. A final question must also be answered: To what extent is Farrug representative of other Maltese villages?

Part—Whole

The contacts of Farrug with the rest of Maltese society can be examined from two points of view. The first focuses on the village as a whole; the second, on the invididuals who make up that whole. Let us take the former first. Contacts exist between Farrug and other social and geographical areas of Maltese society in each major activity field. The part is in contact with the whole through economic, kinship, religious, and political relations. Villagers work outside Farrug, and outsiders work in the village. In the first chapter it was noted that the number of men working outside the village is increasing rapidly. Today, 219 of the 296 working men travel outside the village daily. Most work in the conurbation surrounding the capital. There, they meet persons from many other villages and towns. They are invited to attend special family celebrations and annual festas in other villages. At work they are in touch with persons from all over the island. They exchange news, stories, and notice slight differences between villages. This is a forum where men and, in ever increasing numbers, women from all over the island meet one another and exchange information.

A number of men from other communities maintain regular contact with Farrug because they work there. They include the local police and the parish priest and his family. The two street sweepers, who work their way through the village twice a day to collect rubbish and remove the traces of Farrug's many animals, are also outsiders. Then there is the postman, who also comes twice a day. Finally, there are the scores of hucksters and vendors. They pass through the village in what appears to be a never-ending stream. Wine, kerosene, fish, pots and pans, vegetables, bread, and clothing, all are brought from outside to the village. Some of these outsiders have been in touch with the village for scores of years and have developed fairly intimate contacts with Farrugin. Three policemen stationed in the village married Farrug girls.

Family relations provide another field through which Farrug is in contact with many other villages and towns. There are the many kinship ceremonies—in particular marriages—which bring about a great deal of visiting between villages. The annual festas play a role in this respect. In Farrug no less than 123 households of the 244, that is, just over half, contain at least one person who has married or moved into the village from outside it. These persons retain contact with relatives in their places of birth. Young married couples, for examples, visit their parents at least once a week if they live elsewhere. Native Farrugin and those who have moved into the village visit other villages regularly to see relatives. More than half the households visit a total of 27 different villages and towns almost weekly.

Besides the persons married into the village, there are 35 households from which 51 children still living have married into other villages and towns. These married sons and daughters return frequently to Farrug to see parents, brothers, and sisters. The majority of those who have moved away continue to take a keen interest in the affairs of the village. Here, Pawlu Azzopardi, the president of the Saint Rocco band club, is the most notable example. He has lived outside the village since the early 1930s. He still returns to the village at least once a month for club and family affairs. His visits were more frequent when he was younger. Priests also maintain regular contact outside the village. Dun Frangisk goes regularly to Valletta to see the archbishop and members of the diocesan administration about parish affairs. Every other Wednesday morning he and all other parish priests meet together with the archbishop. In addition, he and Dun Martin serve as confessors and take part in religious ceremonies in other parishes. Through them there is an informal but regular contact with other parishes. There is, naturally, contact with other parishes through corresponding visits from other clerics. Representatives of parish organizations also maintain relations with their counterparts in other parishes. Pietru, for example, travels regularly to Valletta on Catholic Action business. He is a member of the national Catholic Social Guild and attends their weekly meetings at the Catholic Institute in Floriana. MUSEUM members also maintain regular contact with their headquarters in Blata il-Bajda, just outside Hamrun. Farrug is linked to Church bodies all over Malta through its own parish structure.

Various government agencies also link Farrug to the rest of Malta. Notable among these are the police, who maintain a small office and contingent in the village. The department of education has a vested interest in the village. Inspectors call regularly to visit the school and to check the work of the twelve teachers, of whom eight are outsiders who travel daily to Farrug from towns and villages all over Malta. Moreover, twenty-seven Farrugin, of whom twenty-one are boys, travel out of the village daily to attend secondary schools and colleges located, for the most part, in Valletta.

Farrug, of course, has numerous patrons or *qaddisin* outside the village. Some are important landowners. Others are Church officials. Yet others are the influential notaries, lawyers, architects, contractors, and other persons for whom Farrugin work, and to whom they and their close kinsmen submit their problems, ask for advice, help, and interventions with other decision makers. Each family, in general, has access either directly or via third parties to such influential figures. Each professional politician, of course, has a clientele of followers in every village in his district. Farrug is no exception. Many Farrugin assured me that they were good friends with important district political figures. Farrug is also linked to other villages in the district through the administrative apparatus of political parties, particularly the Labour party. Regular political meetings are organized in the village, and outside it. Busloads of Farrug Labour supporters travel to other villages and towns to attend political rallies just before elections. These are usually gay occasions. Farrugin who attend meet relatives and acquaintances from villages all over the island.

In connection with these political links with the outside world, it is well to remember that the village is not represented in parliament as such. There is no political council on which persons represent Farrug as a whole. The representation is partial. Each political party has its own delegates from the village. They, in turn, represent only those Farrugin of their own political color.

There is a final field in which the village maintains relations with the outside world. This, for want of a better term, we may call the "field of recreation." The various village recreative associations represent the village outside it. They also establish and maintain a certain number of contacts. The two band clubs in Farrug are themselves not invited to play at feasts in other villages. It will be remembered that they are band clubs in name only. They have no playing members of their own. However, each club invites other bands to play at its feast. When one of the bands plays for its own annual feast, all bandsmen must be recruited outside the village. These musicians come from all over the island. Each band club is also active in the field of parish politics and maintains a network of extra village relations which help it to out-maneuver its rival. The football club also provides a series of links with other villages. The local team is made up only partly of Farrugin. At least four players come from outside. The president and secretary have dealings with the league officials and leaders of other clubs. The football club also attracts a number of unsavory outsiders to the village before each match. They try to arrange bets and corrupt the players.

The village may be likened to a star, or a point in geographical and social space from which many lines radiate. The lines are qualitatively diverse. Some are geographical. They connect Farrug to other villages and towns. Others are of a higher degree of abstraction. They represent the contacts the village has with various institutional fields of the wider society. They connect the village to the economic, religious, political, and administrative fields. These were examined briefly. The extent and number of these lines has shown that Farrug is very closely linked with the rest of Maltese society.

To what extent is the village as a whole actually connected with and a part of Maltese society? The answer is that the village as such has very few connections. The individuals who make up the village are those who maintain contact with the outside world. The image of Farrug as a star is, consequently, something of a misrepresentation. It indicates that the village itself is the focal point of the various lines which are connected to it. This is not so. We must enlarge the scale, and bring the village itself under the lens of our social miscoscope. We will then note that the lines which radiate from it are, in fact, bundles of relations. The end points of these are connected, not to the village, but to individuals within the village. The village as a unit is connected only very tenuously with the wider society, but through the individuals who inhabit it, it is linked firmly *with* and becomes part *of* wider Maltese society.

The connections between Farrug and the outside world are segmentary. The village as such does not go to work, or visit feasts, or attend wedding receptions. Individual Farrugin do. The football club does not represent the whole village to the outside world, merely its members. The same is true of the band clubs. Each represents about half the village. During the feast and on other ceremonial occasions a band club may pretend to represent the village, and outsiders may accept this, but its right to do so is vigorously contested by the other half of the village. The same is true in the political and religious sphere. In religious matters the parish priest claims to represent the village to the outside world, and the outside world to the village. A few of the most outspoken Labour partisans have turned their backs completely on the Church. They maintain they do not form part of the parish of which the parish priest is the head.

Thus, individuals and groups of individuals, and not the village as such, are the terminal points of the imaginary lines. This change of focus has brought with it an important consequence. This study has focused upon a village, but what has now emerged is the importance of the individual. He, not the village, emerges as the important unit in the process of social communication and cultural integration. Individuals provide the social cement which holds the groups and institutions of society together. Clusters of villages, groups, and institutional fields are interrelated primarily through the individuals of which they are composed. To understand fully the relation between Farrug and the social fabric of Maltese society, it is necessary to complement the village-centered, analytical approach, which must be shifted to include the individual as well.

If we do this we note that each individual is at the center of a network of contacts of different kinds. It is as though the individual were substituted for the village as the focal point for the imaginary lines just discussed. These lines form a network, for they are often interconnected. The institutional fields of kinship, politics, and economics have been arbitrarily separated out in analysis. They are, in fact, closely interrelated. The social network of a person is composed of many different kinds of strands. These are different sets of people with whom he maintains contact because of the different roles he plays. He knows different people as kinsman, worker, neighbor, member of a given band club or political party. Each of these persons has his own personal network of acquaintances recruited from the various institutional fields in which they participate together. Some of these acquaintances are in contact with each other. Others are not. Some, but certainly not all, may be known to the first person. An individual thus stands at the center of his personal network.

He is also a part of the personal networks of many other persons. He can very often ask his direct contacts to put in a good word for him with parts of their personal networks with which he has no contact. The social distance over which a person can send messages for help or information is much larger than the circle of his personal acquaintances. This is an important structural principle. A simple example will make this clearer.

Nina, Pietru Cardona's married sister, wanted a bathroom in her house. Now the government of Malta has a scheme whereby it makes a contribution of about £50 toward the cost of a bathroom for poor families without bathrooms. Nina's mother had recently had a bathroom installed under the scheme, but she had had to give a £5 "present" to a government officer connected with the scheme to have the plans approved. Nina knew all this, but she thought there was another possibility. This was to see if she could not arrange something through one of the links in her network. Although she did not know the officer in charge of the scheme personally, she decided to work through her family physician. This doctor is an important politician for whom she had voted in the past. She went to see him about the matter, and he agreed to help. The officer in charge of the bathroom scheme was, in fact, part of the official network of the family doctor in his role as government official. The doctor asked him, as a favor, to approve the bathroom for Nina without delay. He did so. Nina got her bathroom and it cost her nothing. She would give her vote to her family doctor again in the next election, as would other members of her family. Nina avoided having to give the usual £5 bribe because, unlike her mother, she has an impressive network of contacts. Her beautiful new bathroom is evidence of her ability to use them astutely.

The point I wish to make is that the integration of communities and groups into the whole which we call society takes place via the personal networks of the individuals which constitute them. People are in contact with each other, and through each others contacts, in their turn, with yet other persons. Values are defined, transmitted, and enforced through the chains of linkages in such networks. Information is also exchanged through such personal networks. If Farrug can said to be in touch with the rest of Maltese society, this is so because of the personal networks of its inhabitants. Individual Farrugin are the links between the constituent groups within their village. Through them the village seen as a whole is in contact with, and an integral part of, wider Maltese society.

The danger of an analysis which focuses primarily on the village, in combination with the traditional emphasis upon groups and institutional fields, obscures the role of the personal network. Thus, the important part individuals play in relations between groups, and between groups and the whole, is also obscured. The part is tied to the whole, not through other like parts, but through individuals.

Form and Variation

One final question must be answered. How typical of Maltese villages is Farrug? To try to answer the question I moved for eight months to Kortin, a large Maltese parish the territory of which included two agricultural hamlets. I also carried out a study of fourteen other villages and parishes in Malta and Gozo. I was concerned in this comparative study primarily with what I have called structural form. In comparing Farrug to Kortin in Malta and to Qala in Gozo a number of interesting contrasts emerge. I choose these two villages because I know them somewhat better than the other villages in the comparative sample.

Farrug, as noted, is smaller than the average village. The population of Kortin (including the agricultural hamlets) is 5000, and that of Qala, 1500. In spite of the differences in size, all three have the same administrative apparatus. Each has a police station, a primary school, and a government dispensary open for about an hour a day. Kortin, however, also has a district medical officer stationed in the village. The people of Qala and Farrug must go to a neighboring village to see their district medical officers outside dispensary hours. There is also a considerable difference between them in the occupational classes represented. While Farrug and Kortin have relatively few farmers, 15 and 17 percent of the labor force, respectively, farmers in Qala compose 44 percent of the labor force. In respect to other social distinctions Qala and Farrug resemble one another. Neither has what may be called a class structure. In Kortin, however, there is an exclusive top layer of wealthy, well-educated landowners, businessmen, and professionals. They maintain a style of living and a range of contacts with each other and with persons outside the village which sets them apart from other people in Kortin.

Kortin is the oldest parish and Qala the youngest. The latter split from a neighboring parish towards the end of the last century. It will be recalled that Farrug has two resident priests. Kortin has nine, and Qala, although only a little larger than Farrug, has eight. Farrug has seven religious associations and confraternities, Qala five, and Kortin fourteen. The structure of these villages seen as parishes is, thus, comparable, but they differ considerably with regard to the number of secular associations in each. Farrug has two band clubs and rival festa *partiti*. It also has an active football club and a small but active Labour party committee. Kortin has only one band club and is not divided by festa *partiti,* but it has a football club, a social club, and an active Malta Labour Party club. Qala provides an interesting contrast to the two Maltese villages. It has no secular associations and clubs at all.

In the beginning I was troubled by what appeared to be important differences in the structure of these and other villages. After a time I concluded that three important variables appear to account for the differences. The first is the distance between city and village. I regard this as the most important variable. Kortin is the closest to urban Malta in both geographical and social distance. Qala is the farthest removed. The second variable is the occupational structure. This appears to be a function of the first. The number of persons active in agriculture increases in proportion to the distance from the industrial part of Malta located around the Grand Harbour. The closer the villages are to the latter, the greater the range of occupations and the various social differences which derive from them. This also has a bearing upon the physical size of the villages. An industrial economy can support a larger population than one which is exclusively dependent upon agriculture based upon fixed resource and techniques.

The final important variable I call institutional complexity. This appears to be a function of the first two. The number of associations increases as the distance to the city decreases. This, I believe, is only partly because Sliema and Valletta are centers of innovation. New ideas come into the country through the city. The closer one lives to these areas the more readily one comes into contact with them. Religious and secular voluntary associations multiplied first in areas immediately adjacent to Valletta and Sliema. Moreover, in the villages closest to Valletta there is a greater range of occupations and interests. These find expression in different interest groups and associations. Finally, industrial labor provides more free time and ready cash than does agricultural labor. Free time and cash are ingredients of vital importance if associations and clubs are to flourish. Band clubs have never been established in Malta's smallest and most isolated agricultural and fishing villages (Marsaxlokk, Mgarr, Dingli, Safi, and Gharghur). Moreover, there are only four band clubs in Gozo, two of which are in the island's capital. A contributing factor here is that the Church is also stronger in the more isolated villages. Secular associations such as band and football clubs compete with parish associations for the interest and free time of parishioners. Where it can, the Church has thus used its influence to keep such associations from being established. In Qala, for example, the parish priest and village notables successfully combated several moves to establish a football club. When I asked the headmaster of Qala why he had opposed the club, he replied: "A football club would shift the interest of youths away from the church." He concluded by remarking: "Our church [which had just been completed] would not look the way it does today if there had been that kind of a club here!"

In spite of the differences just discussed, there is, in fact, a remarkable cultural homogeneity. This is, I suggest, the result of the interplay of two important constants. The first is structural and the second cultural. The first thing that strikes the visitor to any village in the islands is the central position of the parish church. As the church soars above the tightly clustered houses, so it also dominates social relations within the village. It has been for centuries the focal point of power and authority within the village, the source from which moral guidance is given. All villages in Malta and Gozo have a concentric layout similar to that of Farrug. The church and the houses of the local notables are on the main square. They form the village core. The periphery is populated by the poorer and less influential villagers. The formal structure of the parish is the same everywhere. This provides the organizational framework of the village.

In all villages in Malta and Gozo there are similar cultural values. To begin with, the language in which these values are expressed is virtually identical. There are no more than insignificant local variations of dialect. Moral values are also remarkably uniform. This is, of course, because of the central position of the Church, and the moral values which the Church teaches. The same applies to the factors on which prestige and class are based. In short, Maltese villagers, whether from large or small villages, have few problems adapting themselves to the customs and rhythm of the life in other villages. The difficulties they encounter come primarily because they are regarded at first as outsiders. The institutional complexity may also be slightly different from that to which they are accustomed. However, as far as language, religion, kinship, and interpersonal relations are concerned, they are on familiar ground.

The remarkable social and cultural homogeneity of Maltese and Gozitan villages is chiefly due to the unifying influence of a strong church in a small relatively isolated island society. The important social differences, which do, of course, exist, lie not so much between the villages themselves. They lie between the villages and Sliema, the modern, anglicized residential suburb for the elite. There is, however, a gradation of differences. Sliema forms one pole of the social continuum in Malta; isolated villages such as Qala form the other. Most villages and towns can be ranged along it in terms of the major structural variables touched on here briefly.

In this final section I have pointed again to a number of important structural variables and constants. The cultural and social principles present in all Maltese villages have been clearly indicated in this case study of one. The way they are combined in Farrug, as in every village, is unique. If this is remembered, then Hal-Farrug can be considered a typical Maltese village.

9

Fieldwork in Malta

Editorial Introduction

Jeremy Boissevain takes us step by step through the sequence of events leading to and through his fieldwork in Hal-Farrug. The preliminary stages of getting to Malta, seeing people and filling out documents, finding a village, then settling in a family of four in improvised quarters, and the initial fieldwork contacts with the people, give us an intimate and useful view of events that are rarely reported in the ethnographic literature. Of particular importance to an understanding of the anthropologist's work in the field is the description of the problem villagers had deciding what he was and why he was in Hal-Farrug. This is always a problem and one that is frequently underestimated by fieldworkers. The anthropologist plays many subroles within the limitations of his overall role as an inquisitive and usually agreeable stranger, so his activities and the reasons for them seem especially confusing. Jeremy Boissevain describes in detail his many daily contacts with shopkeepers, the parish priest, and neighbors. It becomes clear that much of the most valuable data came from unplanned casual contacts. Someone he met on the way to the priest's house, people he met in local bars, others in church, casual contacts in the shops—these provided essential data that cannot be acquired through more formal planned activities. This is one of the truly satisfying aspects of the field experience, but it is also anxiety-arousing since one never knows from day to day and moment to moment whether one will be able to make productive contacts or where they will lead once made. But Boissevain does not neglect the other means for gathering relevant information. The use of current documents, archival resources, photography, direct interviews, genealogies, and census-taking are discussed. And finally, data processing and write-ups are treated, both of which are very instrumental in determining the shape of the case study that students and colleagues will read.

G. and L. S.

Preface

All anthropological research can be divided into four major phases: (1) the preparation for the field, (2) the actual fieldwork, (3) the analysis and writing up, and, last but not least, (4) a period of introspection and reanalysis after the first major work based on the fieldwork has left the researcher's hands. Personally I consider each of more or less equal importance. The preparation and formulation of the questions by the researcher before he sets out into the field influence the sort of data with which he will return. Even a talented researcher using the most sophisticated research techniques will only find the answers to the questions he asks. On the other hand, even if he has excellent data, unless he submits himself and the data to a rather rigid discipline, he will not be able to digest it. Moreover, once digested, it must then be set out clearly and simply so that the reader who knows little or nothing about the problem and area will be able to understand the exposition.

Phase 1 and especially phase 3 are generally given insufficient importance. Yet in terms of input, these demand an investment of at least three or four times as much time and energy as phase 2. I stress this because in this chapter I focus primarily on phase 2, the actual fieldwork. The reader should remember, however, that as far as I am concerned, all phases are of equal importance.

Preparation for the Field

Preparation for my fieldwork in Malta began an unusually long time ahead. It began in fact before I even studied anthropology, when I was still employed as Chief of the CARE[1] Mission to India. The first thing that I did when I learned that I was to be transferred there was to look Malta up in the *Encyclopedia Britannica.* I learned that Malta was in fact an archipelago consisting of four islands, with a total area of just over 120 square miles, situated between Europe and North Africa. Malta, the largest of the islands, is in fact only 17 miles long and 9 miles wide. Though it has been a port of call between the Christian and Moslem worlds for centuries, and its language is a Semitic dialect, the chief features of its culture are European and its people are fervently Roman Catholic. With a population of just under one third of a million, it is the most densely populated country in Europe, if not the world.

At the time Malta was a British Colony, and we met a number of persons in India who had served with the British Armed Services on the island. From them we learned that it was very rocky, hot in the summer, not particularly breath-

---

[1] CARE, The Cooperative for American Relief to Everywhere, Inc., is a nonprofit, nonsectarian, nonpolitical American welfare organization supplying food to large-scale feeding programs. It also provides critical supplies and equipment to technical assistance and community-development programs in various parts of the world.

taking as far as landscape was concerned, and that the people were extremely pleasant. After four and a half fascinating but hectic years in the East, my wife and I both looked forward to a tour of duty in Europe.

The twenty months I spent with CARE in Malta were important for my later

Jeremy Boissevain and the parish priest on the way to the farewell picnic.

research. Although I had learned not a word of the difficult language because nearly all Maltese with whom I came in contact spoke excellent English, I had made a host of extremely useful acquaintances. Moreover, I had learned a great deal about the formal and, to a lesser extent, the informal aspects of the religious, administrative, and political organizations, not to mention the competitive cocktail-party circuits. Moreover, as I discovered later, because of the nature of my work I had an enormous credit of goodwill on which I could draw. The Maltese were extremely grateful for the help that the American people had given them through CARE.

In September 1958 I began two years of intensive training in social anthropology at the London School of Economics and Political Science under Raymond Firth, Lucy Mair, Isaac Schapera, Maurice Freedman, and Paul Stirling. I spent two years there studying not only the principles of social anthropology, but also reading all I could find on Malta and Southern Europe, studying Maltese and formulating my research design and grant application. Reading up on Malta meant working for two days a week in the Colonial Office Library, where I found an excellent collection of books on Malta published in English, French, and Italian, as well as relevant government papers and reports. At the British Museum I was able to trace a lot of incidental references, especially in periodical literature.

My background knowledge on the Mediterranean area was less solid. In the late fifties there was very little sociologically relevant material on this area in print. Moreover, I lacked the time, training, and patience to get the most out of what there was, and my teachers, leading specialists in other areas of the world, were not at home in the literature relevant to this area.

Language was a different problem. It was one which with hard work and concentration I could hope to go a long way toward solving before I actually went into the field. By a stroke of good fortune I met a Maltese headmaster, Francis Chetcuti, studying in London. He lived near us and was prepared to help me with my Maltese for a few hours a week. The study of any language, by whatever means, is hard work. I estimate that I spent at least 320 hours studying Maltese that year. Nonetheless, when I arrived in Malta, I felt I had precious little to show for it. Although by June 1960 I had a vocabulary of somewhere over a thousand words, a fair grasp of the principles of the grammar, and a rudimentary reading knowledge, I had no practice in speaking or listening to it. Francis Chetcuti, in common with all educated Maltese, found it difficult to speak Maltese with a non-Maltese. What I did have, however, as I realized later, was a fairly solid framework on which I could build, and my knowledge of spoken and written Maltese progressed rapidly once we settled in Farrug.

The research problem I became interested in was village-level politics. In particular I had become intrigued through my own experience in Malta by the presence of two competing band clubs in a number of villages. As luck would have it, Francis Chetcuti had been headmaster in several of the southern villages in which this rivalry is particularly acute. One of these villages was Hal-Farrug. As well as my language teacher he became my first informant, and I spent many hours discussing aspects of Maltese society with him.

Hal-Farrug appeared to be ideal. It was small enough so that we could get to know everyone, it was divided by rival band clubs, and I had learned a good deal about it from a friend in Malta. Shortly after New Year 1960 I wrote to a

The parish church and square of Hal-Farrug on a Wednesday morning in November.

friend in Malta, Father Charles Vella, asking if through his network of contacts he could help us locate a house in Hal-Farrug, or in one of the small surrounding villages.

My application to the Colonial Social Science Research Council reflected my interest in local politics and the repercussions at the village level of the national turmoil that had divided all Malta at the time into two hostile camps. Thanks to the support I received from Trafford Smith, a former Lieutenant Governor of Malta then back at the Colonial Office in London, my teachers at the London School of Economics and, particularly from my supervisor, Dr. (now Professor) Lucy Mair, my application was successful.

Full of expectation my wife and I and our two daughters, aged six and four, left England for Malta in our Morris Minor station wagon on Monday, June 27, 1960, camping along the way.

Arrival and First Contacts

We arrived in Malta at dawn on Monday, July 18, 1960 after an overnight trip on one of the expensive and dilapidated little Italian ships that ply between Malta and Syracuse. We were welcomed by Father Charles Vella, and within two hours we were cleared through customs, our car had been unloaded, and we were having breakfast in the Meadowbank Hotel on the Sliema seafront. This was to be our home for the next three weeks.

The next two days were spent getting used to the idea of sleeping in clean sheets on soft beds and seeing to a deluge of official papers. On Wednesday I set out to see if I could find my way to Hal-Farrug. I had never been there before and, like most foreigners living in Malta, as well as a large number of Malta's town-dwelling elite, I did not know my way about the southern villages at all. An entry in my diary for that day reads as follows:

> Went for a drive to Farrug. Got lost and passed through Mqabba. This is quite an interesting looking town. It has about the right "look." Then through to Safi, where a group of ten- to thirteen-year-olds surrounded my car and asked me why I wanted to go to Hal-Farrug, because people there were "savages." The children were friendly enough but tough; they hung about the car for quite a bit. They wanted me to come back and talk to them.

This was my first introduction to the good-natured rivalry between villages and the friendly but aggressive curiosity of village children. There is a Maltese proverb that eloquently sums up this character trait: "God protect us from wild bees and village children." After driving about a bit more I found my way to Hal-Farrug. The diary entry continues:

> Farrug is a small town. It looked cosy. I stopped at a shop for a box of matches and an orangeade. A friendly lady making fishnet in the shop served me. Several boys dressed only in short trousers and undershirts came in to stare at me. I noticed a sign which said Farrug Stars Football Club.

These were the first impressions jotted down in haste and, as is evident, in not nearly enough detail, because those first impressions are extremely important. I had spent fifteen minutes drinking orangeade, smoking a cigarette, and trying my Maltese out on the lady of the shop. The shop turned out to be the football club in which I was later to spend many evenings. The first impressions of Farrug were very positive.

The day after I finally met Dun Gorg, the parish priest of Farrug, who, at Father Charles Vella's request, had located a house for us. The house belonged to Tereza Abela. It was the ground floor of a house in which her daughter Angela and son-in-law Leonard lived. It consisted of a room that opened onto the street, another behind that, and a small room with a sink, which opened onto a little courtyard at the other side of which was a third room which until very recently had been used as a stable. The house was very sparsely furnished and the courtyard was lined with an elaborate system of cages housing chickens and rabbits, and clouds of flies.

The next day I brought my wife along to see it, and we agreed that it had great possibilities. Tereza Abela, who had had some experience renting property she owned in a neighboring town to English Service families, said she would carry out the necessary changes. She promised to paint the stable, arrange for a shower, sink, and toilet, provide beds, a large working table, chairs, and some sort of a sideboard. Carmelo, her eldest son, a skilled electrician at the dockyard, arrived and I was able to discuss a number of technical details with him. Dun Gorg promised to keep an eye on things and assured me that if anyone in the village could, Tereza would see that her boys carried out the work in the fortnight promised. He would see to it that Tereza remained interested in encouraging her boys. We left well pleased at the prospects of finally being able to begin fieldwork in two weeks.

We spent the next twenty days settling down to life in Malta in general, filling in more documents, collecting our trunks, and shopping for the innumerable odds and ends of household equipment that we would need. The logistics of everyday living are in fact a great deal more complicated than those whose life has settled down into a comfortable pattern realize.

Another thing I did was to visit systematically a number of my old contacts with the government. This brought me into the Department of Social Welfare, Department of Information, Central Office of Statistics, University, Department of Agriculture, and law courts. I also made courtesy calls on the Governor and Lieutenant Governor.

I also decided to do something about the infestation of flies attracted to the house by Angela's rabbit and chicken cages. I went along to see the director of the Medical and Health Department, a former CARE contact, and explained the problem of the flies, asking if it would be possible to have the courtyard sprayed with a potent DDT solution. I called back in two days and learned that he had made an appointment for me with the district health inspector. When I met the inspector at our house I had certain misgivings. He was beautifully dressed in a spotless white linen suit and looked quite out of place in the dirty street and, later, in the chaotic house in which the Abela boys were hammering away. When I asked him where the DDT sprayer was, he replied that first he must inspect the house to see if it conformed to public health regulations. After peering in the newly constructed shower stall and into the dark little cupboard which housed the rather battered second-hand toilet, he asked Carmelo a few pointed questions in Maltese. I can still see the inspector, standing in the center of the little courtyard, with a mass of flies settling down densely on his white suit. He told me that the work Carmelo was doing was not only unauthorized, but it was against the regulations: the sinks, toilets, and shower were not properly connected with the sewage system. The landlord must bring the conversions in line with the regulations.

At this point I forgot about the flies and concentrated on getting the immaculate inspector out of the house as quickly as possible. The longer he remained, the slimmer would grow my chances of being allowed to remain in the house which had been found after so much trouble. I was not about to jeopardize my research for a few thousand flies. Fortunately the inspector was easily persuaded to have a cool drink in one of the bars in the village square. I did not ask about DDT anymore. Twenty minutes after he had condemned my house as a menace to public health, he was motoring out of Farrug. We had no more trouble with him. The house remained ours, as did all the flies. Later we had ample opportunity to remember his misgivings about the plumbing system.

Finally the great day arrived. On Saturday, August 6, 1960, at about five in the evening, we moved into our house. Before we knew it, our children were playing happily out on the street with neighboring children, and gazing in awe at the hundreds of goats and sheep streaming back to the houses at sunset. One of the Abela boys came in to ask how things were. He tried, without success, to get the kerosene refrigerator to run. He told us that the music we could hear came from the square. The Saint Martin Band Club was holding a rally to whip up enthusiasm for the coming centenary of their saint. He poked at the refrigerator several more times and then hurried to the square himself.

After tucking the children into their beds in the white-washed stable, which had now become their bedroom, I steeled myself to go to the square. For many months I had been nervously thinking about the moment when I would have to stride across the square in the full gaze of the whole village, and begin my fieldwork. In brief I had a very bad case of stage fright. Unfortunately I had not realized that there was absolutely nothing to be nervous about, for my fieldwork had in fact begun quite some time before.

A few steps beyond our front door I met Salvu, another of Tereza's Abela's sons, with a friend, and together we walked toward the music. The square in front of the Saint Martin's Club was milling with people. Music blared from a loudspeaker stuck in one of the windows. People were clapping and shouting slogans and poems in honor of Saint Martin. Though many were indeed staring at me, I found I did not mind: I was talking to Salvu and his friend. In front of the band club I saw another familiar face, Pietru Cardona, a local school teacher to whom Dun Gorg had introduced me on my first visit. He pulled me into the band club to admire his tape recorder, which was in fact producing the deafening music. Inside I met old Victor Azzopardi, the senior village school teacher, church sacristan and, at the time, treasurer of the Saint Martin Band Club. Though at first reserved, he loosened up at once when I told him I knew Francis Chetcuti, who a few years before had been headmaster in the village. An excited stream of words about band clubs, festa [1] music, different types of fireworks, and how you make them kept washing over me. After a bit I left Pietru and walked with Salvu Abela and his friend through

The author and his oldest daughter, Ieneke, relaxing during fieldwork in Malta.

the village. Though we attracted comments, they were good natured ones. They finally brought me back home. I nodded to Leonard, our upstairs neighbor, who was hiding in the shadow of his doorway listening to a furious quarrel between neighbors a little farther up the street. I learned later that one had hung an enormous picture of Dom Mintoff, the labor leader, over his door. His opposite neighbor objected violently. Fieldwork had begun. The beginning had been painless and pleasant.

[1] A festa is a celebration in honor of a saint. In short, it is the Maltese (and Italian) word for the *fiesta* of the Spanish speaking world.

Adjustment to Hal-Farrug

Although our adjustment to the way of life of our neighbors proceeded rapidly, it was not always without problems. There were basic household problems and new influences that affected our family customs. Besides these, we of course also faced the problem of learning new roles and modes of behavior.

The house was small, but it was reasonably comfortable. It was certainly much more comfortable than the tent in which we had camped for the three weeks previous to our arrival in Malta. Foolishly, we kept comparing, sometimes rather guiltily, our surroundings with the tents and mud huts which we imagined to be typical of anthropological housing in the field. What we forgot was that these would not have been ordinary mud huts placed at random, but the local equivalent of the town houses and mansions of the elite. Applying this principle to Hal-Farrug, we should have maintained a much higher living standard. The focus on peasants, villages, and slums in the sociological literature on southern Europe in general reflects the researchers' inability to keep up with the local elite. It may be possible to study peasants even if you live in a mansion, but if you live in a peasant house it is not possible to meet as an equal those who live in mansions.

Partly as a result of this error, and our recent camping experience, we did little to improve the comfort of our sparsely furnished quarters. The easy chairs remained those of our camping trip: ground-level folding stools. With a few pounds' worth of screening material I ended the constant invasion of flies that almost drove us to despair during the first forty-eight hours. The flies were now confined to the outside, where they continued to attack relentlessly, quickly spotting the laundry on the line and leaving indelible traces on the finish of our car.

The plumbing performed well for the first three weeks and then rebelled. I discovered this as I was having a shower and the neighbors above flushed their toilet. Suddenly I was ankle deep in rebellion. After this I arranged to have the mini-cesspit that served both our houses emptied weekly. In fact most of our neighbors had sewage troubles and the smell of sewage gas was with us everywhere in the village. Fortunately the village is today connected with the main sewage system of the island.

We, or rather my wife, quickly got used to the main problem of housekeeping: the fact that Maltese rise very early. We were anxious to buy as much as we could in the village in order not only to give the business to our neighbors, but also to establish contact. She soon learned to go shopping early, for most of the meat and fresh vegetables were bought up by the women at 5:00 in the morning on their way back from the first Mass. After her first shopping expedition at 8:30, when all she had been able to find were a few bits of meat and some wilted vegetables, she usually set out just before 7:00. It did not take long before she was shouting at the vegetable vendor just like our neighbors, and disdainfully flinging the produce about on his cart in order to get a good bargain. I sometimes think that Maltese vegetable vendors are among the most abused persons in the world. Whenever she had problems concerning shopping she always found a willing escort of women who showed her where she could buy what she wanted.

My new role as a researcher forced us to modify a number of our family customs. I felt obliged to be in the village as much as possible to see what was happening, but I could not always predict when important events would take place. This meant that my coming and going in the family circle was often irregular. My wife had to get used to seeing me disappear in the evening after I had read a story to the children in their stable, which now smelled sweetly of the esparto-grass stuffing their mattresses. Unlike Maltese women, she did not have the network of relatives in the village whom she could visit while her husband was away, though later she did make many friends.

The children made friends quickly with the children of a large farming family opposite us. They, too, had a lot to learn about customs. They especially had difficulty getting used to not accepting biscuits, sweets, and soft drinks eagerly as soon as they were offered. This is considered greedy. They soon learned to refuse politely several times before being convinced to accept the gift. In a short time too they learned songs in praise of the archibishop, and to make rude noises whenever the name of Dom Mintoff was mentioned. Some of their little playmates were rather conservative.

Another problem we had was what I call the two worlds of Malta: town and country. The way of life and the network of contacts that we were building in the villages were completely alien to our upper-class Maltese friends from the towns. But perhaps "problem" is too strong a word. After we moved to Farrug, we dropped out of the sight of many of the acquaintances we had among the town-dwelling elite. A few friends would come and visit us occasionally. Although they never said so directly, the contrast of our sparsely furnished village house with the sumptuous townhouse in which we had once lived was puzzling to most of our Maltese acquaintances. Most Maltese, and especially the competitive professional classes, are intensely materialistic. It was inconceivable to them that someone should *choose* to live in our present surroundings: a tragedy must have befallen us. We saw less and less of them. Maybe this was just as well. The arrival of doctors, lawyers, and ex-cabinet ministers to see us would have troubled the image we were trying to establish. Nonetheless, our very occasional sorties to a nobleman's reception or a formal luncheon with the governor, highlighted the cleavage between the way of life of the villagers and of the town-dwelling professional classes. Equally instructive were the patronizing and disdainful references to Hal-Farrug and villages like it, and to the people who lived there, by the Anglicized upper-classes we met at these functions. The women in particular cooed in their English-accented, Italianized

Maltese at the quaint, rustic way I spoke their language. Although we went to few such functions, those we attended taught us a great deal.

Bringing a large family into the field obviously creates certain problems of adaptation. A good deal of time and energy is invested in the simple logistics of everyday life. These unquestionably take time away from research and writing. Sometimes the combined pressure of the established roles of father and husband plus the new roles the anthropologist is learning and tentatively acting out becomes a considerable strain. Nonetheless the positive advantages gained from having a family in the field far outweigh these disadvantages. To begin with, a family provides an island which is part of another way of life. In Hal-Farrug certainly this prevented me from becoming completely absorbed in local events and helped to maintain a certain objectivity; it also provides companionship. Although the researcher can become close to his informants, he is always an outsider. Research can be a lonely business. Third, a family gives the researcher an adult status. In a society in which all adults are expected to marry, those who produce children (our third daughter was born shortly after we left Farrug!) are regarded as more complete persons. This means that you share this status and the experience that this brings with leaders of the community. Finally, through my wife and children I made a number of extra contacts with neighbors, and gained valuable insights into the world of women.

In short, though we had some problems of adjustment, none were insurmountable. That they were not was in no small measure due to two factors: the flexibility and willingness of the members of my own family to learn new customs and modify behavior and the extreme helpfulness and patience of the people of Hal-Farrug. Within a month or so after our arrival we were no longer *L-Ingliz* and *L-Ingliza,* the generic nicknames given to all foreigners; we became *Gerri* and *Gerrija.* We thus received personal nicknames derived from my Christian name from our neighbors. There were still, however, many problems of adujstment that I had to solve in my role as participant observer.

Participant Observation

The chief research technique of an anthropologist is very different from that of a sociologist. The sociologist works with informants in a research situation, and then retires from the scene. His contacts are generally short and not repeated over time. He knows his informant only in the role of informant. An anthropologist, on the other hand, must be able to get along with people well, for he remains in contact with his informants over a long period of time. He must play many roles before them: not only that of interviewer, but also that of husband, father, neighbor, friend, patron, client, clique-member, and so on. Many of these are new roles for him. Moreover, he must play these roles, whether old or new, in public. In small communities such as Hal-Farrug, the anthropologist, as the newcomer and representative of a foreign culture, is constantly at the center of the village stage. He is consciously acting. After a bit he is usually acting well and receiving compliments from his audience. This is a very heady mixture. The experience of course varies, but it is something that all anthropologists who have done fieldwork share, and in a certain measure it sets them apart from those who have not.

I enjoy fieldwork. Looking back on the work that I have done in my various occupations, it is the close and prolonged periods of contact with people in the field that stand out as high points in my life. Of these the most important was the first.

All anthropologists, I think, are faced with two conflicting roles as participant observers. In Hal-Farrug I felt this very strongly. On the one hand, I wished to construct as large and wide-ranging a network of contacts as possible. On the other, I needed to pursue specific bits of information from selected informants. Although much of the quality of the information I was able to get depended upon the friendships that I had been able to build, the techniques of building those friendships very often got in the way of the information I tried to collect. This is because informants see themselves not as informants but as friends. For the anthropologist they are both. In retrospect, it seems as though I spent many frustrating hours discussing world news with Pietru Cardona—especially the fate of Patrice Lumumba, for the time was 1960—when I would have preferred discussing the band club rivalry, political factions, and gossip relating to key figures I was studying. My relations with Pietru at this stage were not close enough to get this sort of information through prolonged direct questioning. I had to get it indirectly during many hours spent with him and, of course, others, doing things which interested them. With Pietru I discussed Lumumba, with others it was hunting or catching birds, with yet others it was football and drinking.

Later, after many hours of what one might call informant servicing, I developed a few key informants with whom I could retire in private to discuss matters which they did not want others to know they were telling me. I was able to get this information because of the time and energy invested in playing the role of friend and conversationalist. These, and I come back to this, are time-consuming activities. With experience a researcher can learn to be more economical with his time than I was. This depends in part upon his ability to formulate his problem extremely clearly. In no case can he dispense with investing much of his time playing the role of friend to his informants. The information he collects is directly related to his ability to make and maintain friendships among his informants.

There were other new roles that I had to learn to play. One was that of churchgoer. Although we are not Catholic I was determined to go to Mass regularly to hear what was said, to observe who came and where they sat and so forth. Consequently, at 5:45 A.M. on the Monday morning after our arrival, I went to the second of the two daily Masses. Remembering the Mass of the day before, which I had attended from the pavement outside because the church was so crowded, I arrived early to assure a vantage point. There was no one in the church when I arrived, and I sat on the right hand side of the nave, in the third row from the front. Hardly had I settled down when a horde of tittering girls arrived suddenly and surrounded me. I turned uncomfortably around and saw three nuns seated on the aisle. There appeared to be no one else in the church except those around me. It suddenly became apparent that I was sitting in the place traditionally occupied by the nuns and their numerous little charges. After an embarrassed half hour of being observed closely and giggled at intensely, I bolted. Later that day I met Dun Gorg. He discreetly suggested that I sit in one of the lateral apses where the men sat, because it was the custom for the women in the villages to sit in the central nave. I had learned this the hard way. By then I had decided to spend my mornings sleeping and to confine my church attendance to the crowded and important Sunday Mass. I had learned two valuable lessons: to conserve my energy and time as much as possible, and to try and get a description of how I should behave in a given situation before being confronted by it.

The people of Farrug also had adjustment problems. They had a stranger in their midst who was an enigma. I had a family yet I did not go to work like other men. I seemed to be always about, and I asked so many questions. At the outset I explained to the parish priest that I wanted to study all aspects of life in a typical village for my Ph.D. thesis. Yet this information did not circulate widely. When people asked him what I was doing he would try to explain. By no means did everyone ask him, and not all those who did understood his explanation. It soon became apparent that I was remarkably well informed about matters they thought no nonvillager could know. These were simply things such as village nicknames, where people lived, what they did, how many children they had, where they worked, and so on. I certainly did not make it apparent that I knew other more intimate details. There was one man in particular who was troubled. He had heard about me from other people, but never asked me directly what I was doing. He was convinced I was a spy. The problem he and some of his friends faced, as I learned later from Pietru, was to determine for which country I was spying. Because I was American, had studied in England, had a Swedish wife and one child born in Japan, another in Malta, it was not a straightforward matter. He decided finally that I must be a United Nations spy, and began spreading this information about. Pietru told me what was happening and who was responsible. I made a point of meeting the man in his bar. In the course of an evening's hard drinking, for he had an absolutely phenomenal capacity (which I do not), I convinced him that I enjoyed drinking, that I was a student on a very limited budget, that I was genuinely interested in Maltese villagers, that spies usually operate among the town folk, that I had to write a thesis for my teachers, and that he could help me a lot by telling me about his own experience as a leader in the Saint Martin Band Club. The following day I had a frightful hangover, for we had been drinking pint glasses containing a mixture of cheap local wine, beer, and lemonade—a grassroots shandy. I never heard any more about spying.

As participant observer I took part in a wide range of activities. I spent a good deal of the day talking to the shopkeepers and to old men sitting on their doorsteps, and in the evening with the younger men in their cafes, clubs, and on their doorsteps. I also went along on excursions, festas, pilgrimages, weddings, picnics, parties, and receptions in the various clubs. We had Dun Gorg

The author with the chief of the new St. Martin firework factory with the 1967 masterpieces. The one Jeremy Boissevain is holding weighs 20 kilograms.

in to dinner, and after he left the village I often took his successor to the neighboring airport for a drink, a change of scenery, and private conversation. I attended football matches, went hunting, spent a day clap-netting birds, photographed weddings and baptismal parties, went to the fields with farmers, and made the rounds with vendors. In short I saw a lot of the people of Farrug in the various roles they played.

I also systematically pursued a number of key informants: the parish priest, Pietru, old Victor Azzopardi, the sacristan, his brother Pawlu, the president of the Saint Rocco Band Club, the baker and many others. To get systematic information about political matters it was often necessary to see them in privacy. This presented a problem, for the people of Farrug live very close together, and Malta is overpopulated. Moreover Farrugin are reluctant to invite anyone but their closest relatives into their own houses regularly. Exceptions were the parish priest and the shopkeepers. Fortunately Pietru's unmarried sister ran a bazaar and we could talk there in English, which he spoke well. I often went with single informants on picnics or to festas in other villages. Sometimes I drove them into Valletta with me. Occasionally we would simply go for a drive to be alone. Some came to our house, but this gave rise to speculation among the neighbors and the informants were uneasy. In short, our car, brought to provide transportation, in fact also provided important isolation with key informants.

About a month after arrival I began to establish a routine. I got up at 6:00 or 6:30 every morning. Often I would spend a peaceful hour working on my notes before the rest of the family arose. After breakfast, at about 8:00, I left to pick up our car, which was garaged at Tereza Abela's farm on the edge of the village. Normally I went a roundabout way which took me past the parish church, the parish priest's house, the baker's shop, and Pietru Cardona's. It also took me past the main bus stop. All along the way I talked to people, and I always stopped for a chat with Pietru or his sister in her bazaar. This twenty-to thirty-minute swing through the village usually brought me up to date. I then brought the car to the house and my wife brought our eldest daughter to an English-language school in a neighboring town. In the beginning I studied Maltese in the mornings: later I used them to interview the older men who stayed in the village, or to work in the public library in Valletta. Noon was hectic because either my wife or I would have to drive to pick up our daughter for lunch and then return her an hour later, collecting her again at 3:30. In the afternoon I always stayed in the village to work on my notes, and, if the night before had been particularly grisly, I also took a short nap.

Except between 6:30 and 7:30, when I was at home eating and putting the children to bed, I was constantly busy with informants from 4:00 in the afternoon until the clubs and bars closed at about 10:30 or 11:00. After this I would get to work on my notes, first completing my diary and then writing up detailed notes of interviews and observations made during that day. Often I was too exhausted by 12:00 or 12:30 to continue, and would simply jot down an outline of subjects to write up the next day. Sometimes my day's work would end with some scribbled nonsense, an illegible scrawl or an ink blot when I fell asleep over my notes.

An illustration of a more or less average day will perhaps make clearer the rhythm of research. I will not say that it is a typical day, for every day was different. It does, however, illustrate the general attempt to establish and maintain a wide range of links, and to interview certain people more intensively.

Monday, September 19, 1960, started as usual. On the way to pick up the car I learned from Pietru that a number of Requiem Masses were to be held that day in memory of the nineteen-year-old boy electrocuted a year before in one of the quarries surrounding the village. After my wife and daughter left for school, I settled down to study Maltese. After an hour I got fed up and went out to practice it. I went first to the little bazaar of Pietru's sister, where I spent forty-five minutes talking to Pietru's two sisters, his mother, and three customers who came to the shop. I then crossed the street to talk to a farmer, who had come to get a drink in Pietru's cousin's bar. We spent the best part of an hour discussing his farming problems and, of particular importance to me, his reaction to the discussion of the parish priest in church the day before about the financial situation of the Saint Rocco Confraternity. Between 11:00 and 12:00 I worked intensively with the parish priest on my household card system. Dun Gorg liked to display his phenomenal memory and was dictating details of every family in the village: name, nickname, place of birth, age, occupation, band club allegiance and, in passing, choice bits of gossip as well as his personal likes and dislikes.

After lunch, I reviewed the household cards I had prepared with Dun Gorg in the morning, and wrote up the case histories and other information he had provided. (Much later I compared his data to the door-to-door census of my own, and found his to be amazingly accurate.) After my wife and daughter returned home at 3:45, I took the car to the garage to wash it. Carmelo Abela came home at about 4:30. After his tea he came and gave me a hand with the car. When he started to tell me how he had met his fiancée, I began to wax the car to have an excuse to stay with him. As soon as Carmelo left me for his fiancée, I returned home and wrote up the story of his courtship while the details were still fresh (Boissevain 1969: 35–36).

That evening at 8:00, I met Pietru accidentally in front of the parish priest's house. We decided to go for a walk outside the village to find some cool air. At about 9:00 we returned and sat in front of the school chatting. Pietru told me the story of his own courtship and the difficult time he had deciding to break his engagement. We also discussed at great length the evil eye; it had given him a fever the day before. At about 10:30 Pietru went home, and I stopped by his aunt's wine shop. Since only the duty policeman was there chatting to Pietru's cousin, and she obviously was anxious to go to bed herself, I left after fifteen minutes. Although I intended to write up my notes fully, when I got home I found that I was too tired. I simply filled in my diary for the day and outlined the topics to write up the following day. I went to bed at about midnight.

After five months in Farrug, I assumed that the villagers accepted me well enough to give information freely on the delicate matter of political and band club rivalry. In retrospect it was too short a time to assume that sort of confidence. I was still an outsider peering in at the private life of the village. There was still much that people did not care for me to learn. This was especially marked with regard to factional conflicts, which marred the image of village unity that they liked to project to outsiders. I discovered this clearly on Tuesday, 3 January, 1961. The village that day was buzzing with policemen who kept arriving and leaving on motorcycles. In the afternoon I went to Pietru's sister's bazaar to find out what had happened. I casually asked why there were so many policemen in the village. I saw Pietru and his sister exchange glances, and heard Pietru ask in rapidfire Maltese whether he should tell me. His sister shrugged and said I would find out anyway. I chimed in that I agreed, and suggested they tell me now to save time. They burst out laughing and remarked that my Maltese was now so good that they could not keep secrets from me. Pietru and his sister, who was better informed, told how Dun Gorg's coat of arms in the church had been replaced by that of the village sometime during the last two nights, probably on New Year's Eve. Dun Gorg, told about it by phone, had come to Hal-Farrug from his new parish early that morning to verify it, and then reported the damage to the police (Boissevain 1964:1283–1284; 1965:72–73; 1969:63).

To some extent collecting information, especially about matters which many people regard as private, always remains something of a cat-and-mouse game. I had this cat-and-mouse relationship with Pietru until I returned to Farrug the summer of 1967 and hired him as my research assistant. By then I had demonstrated through publications that I needed his help for scientific reasons, and he became much more cooperative.

Other Research Techniques

Besides the participant observation described in the preceding section, I employed a number of other research techniques to gather information on Hal-Farrug. At the public library I systematically went through years of newspapers and yearbooks in order to piece together the background. The newspapers in particular were a useful source of information. The Maltese have acquired from the British the habit of writing letters to the editor. If a village faction fight grows particularly bitter, the weaker party very often tries to wound its opponents by ridiculing them through a letter to the editor. This then gives rise to a furious polemic in which all sorts of fascinating data are made public. In this way I gathered a number of interesting tips on important clashes in Farrug's political past.

The problem of how much time to devote to archives of various sorts is a problem in countries with a long written history. I can offer no rule of thumb. I also consulted some of the parish archives to get vital statistics on deaths, marriages, baptisms. Through contacts established with CARE, I was able to study the police archives pertaining to the village for the past thirty-five years. In addition, I went through records at the Rationing Office, the Electoral Office, and with Rediffusion, the wired sound-broadcasting company. I also, unsuccessfully, advertised in the press and searched the libraries for diaries. It would obviously take me too far afield to discuss the type of information gleaned from the various sources and its relevance. The historical depth given in *Saints and*

Fireworks and *Hal-Farrug,* as limited as it is, would not have been possible without this search. On the other hand, I wasted much time on archives as I did not always know what I was looking for, especially in the beginning. In order to carry out such research economically I should have had a much more sharply formulated research design than I had.

In the beginning in Hal-Farrug I made extensive use of my camera to connect names to faces. I photographed many crowd scenes, and later asked informants to identify the persons. One of the most useful pictures in this respect was the portrait of the Saint Martin partisans posing proudly with the mountain of fireworks they prepared for the centenary of their Saint (Boissevain 1969:73). People would tip me off when interesting things were going to happen, and, if crowds were present, see that I got a ringside seat with a running commentary. Although there was also a keen photographer in the village who earned a bit of extra money with his hobby, we did not really compete. I only charged the cost price on my pictures, which for the most part were scenes in which he was not particularly interested. The camera also was a convenient means of getting me invited to intimate family celebrations, such as bethrothal parties, where a regular village photographer would have been an uncomfortably familiar figure. Although once an avid amateur photographer, I soon found that taking really good photographs is incompatible with being a good anthropologist. Both are full time occupations. Moreover the best angles are often far from informants.

Direct interviews of course were one of the chief techniques I used. I had interviews with the various village leaders, association officers, living former village parish priests and police officers, politicians who had canvassed in the village, and many more. Many of these interviews were formal in the sense that I had made appointments for them. Many were also accidental, such as the interviews with Carmelo Abela and Pietru Cardona described above. If I could, I always spent some time before an interview preparing it and thinking through the questions, making sure that I had them firmly in my head. Very often I would jot down key words with a ballpoint on my palm or, more usually, on a page in my pocket notebook. In the course of the interview I would elicit a date or an address which gave me an excuse to open the notebook so that I could jot down trigger words to remind me later of the subjects discussed. Once the notebook was open I could also unobtrusively check the prepared list of questions to make sure that I had covered all the planned subjects. An interview with untrained informants, especially if you are after information he is not too eager to part with, has a way of branching out along unforeseen paths. Later it is surprisingly difficult to remember the different topics discussed.

Genealogies were a help in learning how the villagers were related to each other. I collected ten extensive genealogies which were sufficient to place everyone in the village. Genealogical data I collected on the census provided further information. Because I was not particularly interested in kinship at that time, the genealogical data I have on Hal-Farrug is rather thin. Later, in the summer of 1968, I was to collect a giant genealogy from Pietru Cardona, who has over 400 living relatives of his generation. This, however, belongs to a later period of research.

I conducted the village census in the fourth month. For many days I procrastinated whether it would be worth the effort. Finally I decided it would be, and that I should do the work myself and not try to get someone else to do it. The data I collected related primarily to household composition, occupation, and membership in the various associations. Although I tried to get information on extra sources of cash income and land ownership, this made people suspicious. Since the economic data they then gave was extremely unreliable, I soon stopped asking for them, fearing that it would jeopardize my relations with the villagers. Even my neighbor Leonard, Tereza Abela's son-in-law, did not want me to note down that he supplemented his dock yard policeman's salary by buying and selling eggs and poultry.

It is important to remember that I was in Malta during a time of political crisis (1960–1961). Questions which were related to politics were difficult to pose. Many persons did not wish to disclose their true political sympathy for many reasons. Those who supported the Labour Party were afraid of being branded as communist heretics by the faithful; some were afraid of losing their jobs; yet others were afraid of generating conflict with family or neighbors. Another sensitive subject I have already mentioned was allegiance to a particular festa faction. For this reason I did not include direct questions relating to political or festa faction affiliation on the census. In this small community it was of course possible to get this information, as well as that on extra sources of income, indirectly.

Once I stopped asking about money, I was welcomed into most of the 244 households. The few exceptions were houses in which mentally disturbed members of the household were confined. The success of the census was in no small measure due to the way in which Dun Frangisk announced from the pulpit that I was going to every household to ask some harmless questions. In fact, in most of the houses where I called, the problem was not reserve but overfriendliness. Many thought of my visit as a social occasion and offered me the glass of whisky that good manners demanded. Moreover many gave me eggs, soft cheeses, and tomatoes. I often had to dash home to keep my pockets from bursting, and once I had raw egg slithering down the inside of my leg. The census took eleven days. By the second day I had developed a confidence and smoothness which made me feel a little silly about the hesitation I had had about carrying out the survey.

On the 8th of January we moved from Farrug to Kortin, where we lived until we left Malta in September. The object of the move was to gather comparative information on a larger village and one that was not divided by band club rivalry. Although I intended to return to Hal-Farrug after three months, the house was no longer available when we wanted to move back. Tereza Abela and her sons had moved into it, leaving her husband, with whom she had quarrelled, to look after the farm. Though I continued to visit Hal-Farrug regularly to attend a number of the important functions, including many weddings, participant observation in the village was obviously reduced to a minimum. Later a research assistant and I made short comparative studies of the general organization, leadership, and patterns of conflict in twelve other communities. Much later, during the summer of 1967, thanks to the generosity of the Wenner-Gren Foundation for Anthropological Research, I was able to revisit Hal-Farrug to bring myself up to date. Pietru provided me with very valuable assistance, as did a number of others, including the new parish priest. Some of the data I collected at this time found its way into *Hal-Farrug*.

Processing the Data

One of the most critical phases of fieldwork is processing the voluminous data collected. I received little systematic instruction on this during my graduate work. Though I heard vague descriptions of how anthropologists processed their data, the only "anthropologist's field notebook" I was actually able to touch and look at, and this only after many unsuccessful requests, was one of Malinowski's old field notebooks from the Department's museum. From Paul Stirling I heard how John Barnes kept his notes. Since this seemed an economical method I decided to adopt it myself.

I used a variety of notebooks. To begin with I had a little pocket notebook with a hard cover and a pencil, which I carried with me always. In this I jotted down odd bits of information during interviews, and more detailed outlines of the subjects discussed as soon as informants were out of sight. I also kept a second one in which I systematically put down the meaning of new words I heard; unfortunately I discontinued this after two months. I used a stenographer's notebook for formal interviews when I knew I could write, and for all genealogies, for copying data from the police records, and for rough notes from newspapers and other archives. Finally I had a series of much larger notebooks which I kept under lock and key in our house. Into these I wrote up in detail interviews and personal observations, some points of which I had usually jotted down in my pocket or stenographer's notebook. The lined pages were numbered consecutively and I ruled in a large margin on the left hand side. The entries were made chronologically. In the margin I wrote the headings under which the entry could be indexed. Following Paul Stirling's advice, I indicated as many possible headings as I could. These headings and subjects were consolidated in three central indexes at the back of each notebook: events and subjects peculiar to Hal-Farrug, names of people, and events and subjects of general importance. Every day I tried to bring this index up to date, cross-referencing where necessary. While in the field I did not allow myself enough time to do this properly.

Besides these notebooks I also kept a daily diary into which I entered appointments and a rather terse summary of persons and places visited during the day. This was a chore which I did not do in great enough detail, but I did do it faithfully. The importance of this diary had rightly been stressed repeatedly at the field seminar in London. It provides a rough structure to the subject matter in the notebooks, as well as a record of how I spent my time, and whom I saw on what occasion. I had separate notebooks for Gozo, where I carried out a certain amount of research, and for the detailed notes which I took from library books. I indexed them all in the same way.

As already indicated, I developed a card system which provided data on household composition, occupation, nicknames, political allegiance, band club affiliation, and place of birth of each member. This card system, set up with the help of the parish priest at the end of the first month in Hal-Farrug, was invaluable, and I constantly drilled myself with the names, addresses, nicknames, and occupations of the village's 1300 inhabitants. Even today I still remember this information, and on return visits recently I have again, I fear, raised the spectre of the spy with it.

Besides notebooks and cards I had a system of folders for various activities, certain persons, genealogies, and subjects such as kinship, godparenthood, church organization, and so on. I placed these upright in a cardboard box. Into these I filed pamphlets, texts written by villagers, sheafs of notes, pictures and newspaper cuttings. I also had a growing collection of government departmental reports, pamphlets, statistical abstracts, and census reports to which I made constant reference in my comparative work.

Fortunately the Colonial Social Science Research Council required its research fellows to make an interim report after the first half year. I did this when I moved to Kortin. I began consolidating my notes on Friday, January 13. A month later I posted the report, a 14,000-word paper on local politics in Hal-Farrug, to the Colonial Office and to Dr. Lucy Mair, my supervisor at the London School of Economics. It had been a busy month. I first worked out the statistical results of the house to house census. This was a particularly time-consuming piece of work. I also indexed my notes, thought through a number of basic problems, and made plans for the rest of my research. I could not, however, work on the report continually: The sewage problem again arose and the plumbing could only be manipulated through the floor of the converted chicken house I was using as my study. There were also many more general problems of settling into a new village. Writing the report forced me to rethink basic problems and look at my material in terms of those problems. In doing so I discovered numerous shortcomings in my material. Moreover, because I now had a written piece, I was able to elicit valuable criticism and comments from my supervisor and her colleagues at the London School of Economics. This feedback was invaluable.

Two months later I again took time off from actual research and retired to a friend's summer house in Saint Paul's Bay for a week. Isolated from family, neighbors, and informants, I again indexed notes, read my material through, took stock of where I was, and where I still had to go. Unfortunately I did not write anything. Finally, I must mention that I had valuable discussions on many aspects of my fieldwork as well as some of my findings with friends and persons outside the villages. Most of these were what could be called, quasi-academics, that is, they were persons who had certain academic interests but who were not even part-time academics. They included a government secretary who was an expert on folklore, employees of the library who knew where the books I needed were placed (many were not cataloged!) and who had done considerable private research for Sunday supplement articles and pamphlets, a priest who was conducting pastoral research, a police sergeant interested in folklore, and many more. These, unlike most at the university, were keenly interested in my research and offered many insights, as well as access to their clipping files and records.

Foolishly, I did not show them my interim report, and thus missed the feedback this would have provided. The reason I did not show it is perhaps partly due to the way my research was sponsored. I was working with funds received from the British Government via the Colonial Social Science Research Council. As political relations between Malta and Britain at the time were very delicate, I felt most awkward about my sponsorship. I therefore did not disclose the exact source of funds unless I was pressed to do so, preferring merely to note that a British institution had sponsored me. Had the true nature of the source come out, I was sure, and still am, that my relations with Malta Labour Party officials would have been much less cordial than they were. Consequently, I had always the slightly embarrassed feeling that I was there under false colors. This of course was foolish, for the area of research and the problems on which I was working were completely those of my own choosing, not those of the British Government. Nonetheless, the feeling persisted, and I was not as forthright about my work as I should have been, and have since become.

Analysis and Writing Up

We returned to London by air in the middle of September 1961. I took with me my notebooks containing some 1500 pages, some 360,000 words of notes, plus the household cards of Hal-Farrug and Kortin. The rest of my data—pounds of books, papers, surveys, and cards—followed by ship. Fortunately we were able to move into a furnished house. This meant there were few settling in problems and I was able to begin work immediately.

The first task was of course to complete my indexing. I expanded certain sections of the index. Using these new categories I reread all my notes, indexing as I went along. This task, as I remember it, took about two weeks of intensive, tedious work. After that I began writing. I was determined to deliver my final report to the Colonial Office by the time my research grant ran out in the end of November.

Mondays through Saturdays, I worked flat out from 7:00 in the mornings to about 10:00 at night, with four hours off for meals and playing with the children. On Friday mornings, however, I went to Professor Raymond Firth's seminar at the London School of Economics, where in the course of the year I gave several papers. Since I did not have the resources to continue after the summer, my thesis had to be completed before August 1962. I could not afford the luxury of going to any of the other interesting research seminars at the L.S.E.

The third week in November I presented Dr. Mair with a 25,000-word typescript. She gave it very severe criticism, and I spent the next two weeks rewriting and editing it before I passed it on to the typist. With considerable satisfaction I delivered the required three copies to the Colonial Office around the middle of December. These apparently disappeared into the great maw of the dying colonial apparatus and, as far as I have been able to gather, were never looked at again by anyone. They apparently never reached Malta. A year later I had to lend my personal copy to Sir Maurice Dorman, the new Governor of Malta!

My supervisor's criticism of the final report, if anything, was even more severe than of the first draft. I took her pungent but most instructive marginal comments to heart and began work on my thesis. The first chapter required a good bit more historical research and I journeyed back and forth to the Colonial Office Library a number of times. That chapter gave me a good bit of trouble, and not surprisingly, it was rejected twice by Lucy Mair. I then worked methodically through each of the nine chapters, revising where necessary after sessions with my supervisor. I finished in the beginning of July, and in August left for a research post in Sicily, returning to London briefly in November for the examination of the thesis.

Hal-Farrug, of course, grew out of this initial research and my first book, though I did not return in my writing to Malta until 1967. During this period I carried out research in Sicily, prepared and taught my first courses at the Université de Montréal, moved from Canada to England, and from there to Holland. At the University of Amsterdam I lectured on Hal-Farrug from January to June 1967. That summer I returned to Malta to discuss certain points with friends and briefly to restudy the village. Using my lecture notes I then dictated the manuscript for Hal-Farrug. My secretary in Holland typed out the tapes. During the Christmas break I revised the manuscript, rewriting extensively. It was then stencilled and, in February, sent for comment to the Spindlers, who were in Europe at the time, and to friends in Holland, Malta, and England. The final manuscript was sent, together with pictures, diagrams, and maps, to the publisher the beginning of May 1968.

The Wisdom of Hindsight

If I were to carry out the research in Hal-Farrug again, would I set about it in the same way? Not completely in the same way, I think. To begin with, I would not try to divide my time over two villages. It could be argued that in terms of my objectives—a comparative study of village politics—this was not particularly unsatisfactory. The trouble was that I learned much about many villages but not enough about one.

Another shortcoming was that my research problem was not clearly enough formulated when I went into the field. Of course it is an open question whether an inexperienced researcher fresh from graduate school can ever hope to achieve the economy of action of an experienced researcher. Moreover, the theoretical apparatus available on village-level politics in the late fifties and early sixties was remarkably thin (Easton 1959). On the other hand, besides lacking clear concepts as to just what the political field was—and there were important books on the subject that I had not read—I naively expected to find groups within groups. My lack of critical attention to the basic theoretical premises concerning the nature of society postulated by social anthropologists, most of whom, following Evans-Pritchard (1940:262), saw the social structure as the "relations between groups of persons within a system of groups," ensured that I was ill-prepared to observe, let alone analyze, the networks and shifting coalitions of individuals I was in fact confronted with. The disproportionate amount of time I spent making the rounds of village associations and participating in their activities, in spite of the fact that their members represented but a fraction of the total population of the village, can be attributed partly to my misconception about the nature of society. I saw these associations as the formal groups which I had been trained to think would provide the key to the social structure. They did not. It took a long time to escape from the simplistic, group-dominated functionalist model I used as my primary analytical tool in 1960 (Boissevain 1968). *Hal-Farrug* therefore has a very different theoretical orientation than my first book.

I am sorry too that I did not spend more time systematically collecting local expressions and categories of thought. Because of this my knowledge of Maltese, while eminently serviceable for conversation and reading, remains rudimentary.

Since my first research in Hal-Farrug, I have developed another system of note-taking. Briefly, I type each entry in triplicate on a separate card, indexing not only the cards but various subjects covered. I now also spend much more time working out the notes. In Farrug I foolishly felt guilty about spending more than two or three hours a day on my notes; often I spent even less. I assumed that I had to be where the action was, not realizing that unless what is observed is digested thoroughly while in the field, it loses meaning and therefore value once you leave. You can only do this properly if you spend approximately one third of your time in the field processing your notes and writing.

Another shortcoming was that I did not do nearly enough writing. I should have been consolidating my data frequently in short reports. One of the reasons I spent more time on my interim report than I should have, was because my writing was rusty, and my data scattered and undigested. Yet this report remains the most valuable single exercise I carried out while I was in Malta. It is only when an anthropologist sets down his observations and analyses these clearly for himself and others that he becomes aware of the lacunae. If he does this in the field he can still do something about it. By consolidating his data at regular intervals, he will leave the field with much material already worked out and on paper. Much of this can be placed without alteration in the final report. A number of tables and sections I used in *Saints and Fireworks* and *Hal-Farrug* were lifted verbatim from the report to the Colonial Office that I prepared in my chickencoop in Kortin.

These then are some of the things that I think I have learned from my experience in Hal-Farrug, as well as elsewhere in the years since I carried out my research there. Nonetheless, in spite of my shortcomings and greenness, or perhaps because of them, the five months spent in Hal-Farrug will always stand out as my most important experience as a researcher.

References

Boissevain, Jeremy F., 1965, *Saints and Fireworks: Religion and Politics in Rural Malta*. London School of Economics Monographs on Social Anthropology No. 30. London: The Athlone Press (Revised paperback edition, 1969).

———, 1968, The place of non-groups in the social sciences. *Man* (N.S.) 3:542–556.

———, 1969, *Hal-Farrug: A Village in Malta*. New York: Holt, Rinehart and Winston, Inc.

———, 1970, *The Italians of Montreal: Social Adjustment in a Plural Society*. Ottawa: The Royal Commission on Bilingualism and Biculturalism.

Easton, David, 1959, Political Anthropology. In Bernard J. Siegel, ed., *Biennial Review of Anthropology*. Stanford, Calif.: Stanford University Press, pp. 210–262.

Evans-Pritchard, E. E., 1940, *The Nuer*. Oxford: The Clarendon Press.

10

1979 Epilogue

"Back in 1966, when I arrived, the village was like a monastery. It was closed to the outside world. Now, like a piazza, it is open to the outside. People only come here to sleep and eat." This is how Hal-Farrug's ex-parish priest, Dun Ang Vella, described the changes of the past decade. The pace of change in Malta has indeed been rapid. Everywhere there are new houses and roads. There are new factories and literally scores of new hotels, for Malta has become one of the fastest growing tourist centers in the Mediterranean (Boissevain 1977c, 1979a, b). Between 1968 and 1978 tourist arrivals rose from 137,000 to 478,000. Politically, too, the country has changed. Since 1971, it has been governed by the socialist Malta Labor Party, which has systematically severed traditional military and economic links with northern Europe and cultivated relations with Arab states, particularly Libya. It has also curtailed the power of the church, limited the influence of the professional classes, and provided considerable help to underprivileged social groups (1975, 1977b).

In Hal-Farrug these changes are apparent. New access roads were built to by-pass the enormous new airport runway, which in turn gobbled up most of the choice agricultural land that survived World War II airfield expansion. At the edge of the village a foreign-owned electronic factory, built in the late 1960s, provides work for 200 girls from surrounding villages. Now virtually all girls over 16 who have left school work outside the village, as do increasing numbers of married women without children. Though the position of women in Malta has improved slightly in the past decade, the husband is still legally the head of the house and his wife may not fully administer her property. There is now, in principle, equal pay for equal work, but discrimination still persists: Women employed by government and many private firms are contractually obliged to terminate employment upon marriage. If needed, some are temporarily reemployed at lower salary and without pension rights. While women's organizations are active at the national level, there is no evidence in Hal-Farrug of feminist activities. On the other hand, girls are far better dressed than a decade ago, they can spend more money and, increasingly, are free to leave the village in the evening by bus or a boyfriend's car (1973, 1978a).

The growing outward orientation has helped blur the sharp distinctions between town and country. Though their village accent is still evident, the dress and manners of young Farrugin are now almost indistinguishable from those of townsmen.

New housing came to Hal-Farrug later than to most villages. There is now a government housing development, and some better-off villagers have built smart houses on the outskirts. In a sense, this contradicts the church-centered, concentric residential pattern discussed in Chapter 5. Following the building boom of the late 1960s sparked off by tourists and foreign residents, people everywhere began to build large houses in rural areas adjacent to the main centers. These rapidly became choice residential areas. This also took place in Hal-Farrug; the changing settlement pattern thus reflects increasing Farrugin involvement in the goings-on beyond the parish. Their new houses no longer face the main square and the parish church, but look outward, towards the rest of Malta (1978a).

Just as the church no longer forms the exclusive focus of the village as a geographical unit, so its position in Maltese society has also changed. Malta has increasingly felt the secularizing impact of industrialization, tourism, television, and the relaxation of press and film censorship. Other forms of entertainment draw Farrugin away from the traditional feasts and rituals. Literate villagers depend less upon the parish priest to interpret forms and mediate with the authorities. In varying ways these developments have weakened the power of the church. But we must not exaggerate. Dun Ang explicitly noted that Farrugin had still made extensive use of him to cope with the growing flood of government forms and regulations. Nonetheless, the long-term trend is evident (1977a, b).

The Labor government has also taken steps to reduce the church's power. Members of the clergy can now be punished severely for interfering with elections as they did in the past. It also introduced civil marriage, taxed religious bodies, abolished many traditional feast days, and obliged school chaplains to hold traditional religious services after school hours. In short, besides limiting the church's power, the Labor government has also humiliated it. Though the wounds caused by the confrontation with the church (set out in Chapter 7) have closed, they are still tender. Many Farrugin took pains to remind me how they were persecuted for their political convictions in the early 1960s.

Having said this, it is fascinating to note that despite these secularizing influences, Farrug's annual *festas* are better attended, noisier, and more colorful than they were in the 1960s. Why is this so? To begin with, *festas* draw greater crowds now because public transport has improved and because tourists enjoy *festas*. Because of tourist interest, many Maltese who once avoided what they regarded as "low class," "quaint" celebrations, now visit them because they have come to regard them as part of their cultural heritage. National culture is important to new nations (Boissevain 1977c and 1978a). *Festas* have also grown because of increased welfare. People can spend more money to celebrate. Every year Farrugin add decorations; large cardboard lions, blue and red scarfs, and colored umbrellas have now become part of Farrug *festa* culture. The greatest *festa* innovation in Hal-Farrug was the introduction of an exuberant noon band march on the day of the feast. This leaves fervent Farrugin so limp that they can hardly greet their saint when he emerges from the church in the evening.

There are several other reasons why the scale of feasts has grown. The Saint Rocco band, dormant since the massive emigration of the 1950s, was rejuvenated by an active, in-marrying bandmaster. This fanned competition, as did the inauguration in 1975 of Saint Rocco's new platform. In 1978, the *partit* celebrated the centenary of the foundation in Hal-Farrug of the Confraternity of Saint Rocco. Competition during the celebration reached such a pitch that my friend Pietru Cardona (1974b: 97–147) felt more comfortable watching the procession from his mother's roof. The street was no place for a staunch Saint Martin supporter.

There is yet another reason for the growth of *festa* enthusiasm in villages divided by *festa partiti*. In 1975, Labor politicians ordered police not to enforce the 1934 church regulations that severely curtailed the celebration of secondary feasts. Thus the lid was taken off *festa* competition. In Hal-Farrug, Saint Rocco supporters set about renewing and expanding their stock of street decorations. Saint Martin followers, of course, followed suit. It seems that the decline in band club rivalry that I predicted in 1968 (pp. 90–91) has most definitely not come about! (See also 1974a, b, and 1978b.)

Not only has the pitch of parish politics risen. Tension in the national political arena is also high. Malta now seems permanently on the eve of an election, for there is bitter confrontation between the ruling Malta Labor Party and the Nationalists, the opposition party. Farrugin take politics seriously. National politics still form points of cleavage within the *festa partiti*, while these in turn divide along political party lines. This affects band club solidarity just before the elections, and empties the popular new Labor club during a *festa*.

In spite of the growing involvement of Farrugin in the world outside the parish, their gossiping, rivalry, rituals, and festivals have ensured that Hal-Farrug has remained a community in every sense of the word.

Bussum
May 1979.

References

BAILEY, F. G., 1969, *Stratagems and Spoils*. Oxford: Basil Blackwell.

BANTON, MICHAEL, 1965, *Roles: An Introduction to the Study of Social Relations*. London: Tavistock Publications.

BARTH, FREDERIK, 1966, *Models of Social Organization*. London: Royal Anthropological Institute.

BOISSEVAIN, JEREMY F., 1965, *Saints and Fireworks: Religion and Politics in Rural Malta*. London School of Economics Monographs on Social Anthropology No. 30 (see Recommended Reading list).

——, 1967, Some Notes on the Position of Women in Maltese Society. *In* J. G. Peristiany, ed., Proceedings of the 1966 Mediterranean Sociological Conference. Athens: Social Sciences Center.

——, 1973, Some Notes on the Position of Women in Maltese Society. *In* Knut Weibust, ed., *Kulturvariation I Sydeuropa*. Copenhagen: NEFA Forlag, pp. 125–143.

——, 1974a, Conflict and Change: Establishment and Opposition in Malta. *In* J. Davis, ed., *Choice and Change: Essays in Honour of Lucy Mair*. London: The Athlone Press, pp. 17–43.

——, 1974b, *Friends of Friends: Networks, Manipulators and Coalitions*. Oxford: Basil Blackwell.

——, 1975, Islands on the Move: Social Trends in Malta, 1960–1974. *Cobweb* 7: 7–13.

——, 1977a, When the Saints Go Marching Out: Reflections on the Decline of Patronage in Malta. *In* E. Gellner and J. Waterbury, eds., *Patrons and Clients in Mediterranean Societies*. London: Duckworth.

——, 1977b, A Causeway With a Gate: The Progress of Development in Malta. *In* Sandra Wallman, ed., *Perceptions of Development*. Cambridge, Eng.: Cambridge University Press, pp. 87–99.

——, 1977c, Tourism and Development in Malta. *Development and Change* 8: 523–538.

——, 1978a, The Maltese Islands. *In* Ann Sutherland, ed., *Face Values*. London: BBC Publications, pp. 108–139.

——, 1978b, Of Men and Marbles: Notes Towards a Reconsideration of Factionalism. *In* M. Silverman and R.F. Salisbury, eds., *A House Divided: Anthropological Studies of Factionalism*. Memorial University of Newfoundland, pp. 99–110.

——, 1979a, Tourism and the European Periphery: The Mediterranean Case. *In* Dudley Seers, Bernard Schaffer, and Marja-Liisa Kiljunen, eds., *Underdeveloped Europe: Studies in Core-Periphery Relations*. Hassocks, Eng.: The Harvester Press, in association with the Institute of Development Studies, University of Sussex, pp. 125–135.

——, 1979b, The Impact of Tourism on a Dependent Island—Gozo, Malta. *Annals of Tourism Research*.

BOTT, ELIZABETH, 1957, *Family and Social Network: Roles, Norms, and External Relationships in Ordinary Urban Families*. London: Tavistock Publications.

FRIEDL, ERNESTINE, 1962, *Vasilika: A Village in Modern Greece*. New York: Holt, Rinehart and Winston, Inc. (see Recommended Reading list).

MIÈGE, M., 1841, *Histoire de Malte*. 2 vols. Brussels, Belgium: Gregoir et Wouters.

PITT-RIVERS, J. A., 1954, *The People of the Sierra*. London: Weidenfeld and Nicolson (see Recommended Reading list).

YOUNG, MICHAEL and PETER WILLMOTT, 1957, *Family and Kinship in East London*. Baltimore: Penguin Books.

Recommended Reading

Cultural Area

BANFIELD, EDWARD C., 1958, *The Moral Basis of a Backward Society*. New York: Free Press.
A short, provocative, but ethnocentric analysis of factors which impede community action in a village in Lucania, in southern Italy.

BOISSEVAIN, JEREMY, 1966, Poverty and Politics in a Sicilian Agro-Town. *International Archives of Ethnography*, 50:198–236.
A short account of values, structure and local politics in a Sicilian town of 20,000.

CAMPBELL, J. K., 1964, *Honour, Family and Patronage: A Study of Institutions and Moral Values in a Greek Mountain Community*. New York: Oxford.
A detailed study of the value system of an isolated sheepherding community. It is the most penetrating study of its kind of a Mediterranean society.

FRIEDL, ERNESTINE, 1963, *Vasilika: A Village in Modern Greece*. New York: Holt, Rinehart and Winston, Inc.
An account of a very small farming community at the foot of Mount Parnassus. It provides a detailed analysis of the dowry system.

KENNY, MICHAEL, 1961, *A Spanish Tapestry: Town and Country in Castile*. London: Cohen and West.
An interesting study that contrasts a remote village to a parish in Madrid.

LISON-TOLOSANA, CARMELO, 1966, *Belmonte de los Caballeros: A Sociological Study of a Spanish Town*. New York: Oxford.
A probing contemporary and historical analysis of a small town in Aragon that gives a particularly detailed account of stratification and religion.

PERISTIANY, J. G., ed., 1965, *Honour and Shame: The Values of Mediterranean Society*. London: Weidenfeld and Nicolson.
A series of perceptive studies which deal with an important theme in Spain, Greece, Cyprus, Kabylia, and among Egyptian Bedouin.

PITT-RIVERS, J. A., 1954, *The People of the Sierra*. London: Weidenfeld and Nicolson.
A pioneering study of an Andalusian village by the *doyen* of anthropologists who write on southern Europe.

——, ed., 1963, *Mediterranean Countrymen: Essays in the Social Anthropology of the Mediterranean*. Paris: Mouton.
Twelve important studies on different aspects of societies bordering on the Mediterranean.

STIRLING, PAUL, 1965, *Turkish Village*. London: Weidenfeld and Nicolson.
An excellent study of two changing villages in the non-Christian portion of Mediterranean Europe.

WOLF, ERIC R., 1966, *Peasants*. Englewood Cliffs, N.J.: Prentice-Hall.
A brilliant short introduction to the study of peasant societies everywhere.

Malta

AQUILINA, JOSEPH, 1961, *Papers in Maltese Linguistics.* Malta: The Royal University of Malta.

A collection of essays by the leading authority on this unusual language.

———, 1965, *Teach Yourself Maltese.* London: The English Universities Press.

For enthusiasts—the only available introductory work on Maltese, a difficult language.

BLOUET, BRIAN, 1967, *The Story of Malta.* London: Faber.

A concise, readable account of the islands' physical, economic, and constitutional history from prehistoric times to the date of its publication.

BOISSEVAIN, JEREMY, 1965, *Saints and Fireworks: Religion and Politics in Rural Malta.* London School of Economics Monographs on Social Anthropology No. 30. London: Athlone Press.

An analysis of the interplay between parish and national politics just before Malta achieved independence.

BOWEN-JONES, H. DEWDNEY, J. C., and FISHER, W. B., eds., 1961, *Malta: Background for Development.* Durham, England: Department of Geography, Durham Colleges in the University of Durham.

A collection of twenty-seven specialized articles on different aspects of the social and physical geography of Malta and Gozo.

BUSUTTIL, E. D., 1949, *Kalepin (Dizjunarju): Malti-Ingliz.* 2d. ed. Malta: Progress Press.

———, 1948, *Kalepin (Dizjunarju): Ingliz-Malta.* Malta: Giov. Muscat.

The only Maltese-English dictionaries in print. They are usable, but not very good.

CASSAR-PULLICINO, J., 1966, Notes for a History of Maltese Costume. *Maltese Folklore Review,* 1: 149–216.

One of the many essays by the foremost authority on Maltese folklore. It also contains a useful bibliography of many early travelers' accounts of Malta.

EBEJER, FRANCIS, 1958, *A Wreath for the Innocents.* London: MacGibbon & Kee.

A novel of romance between a young nobleman and the daughter of a wineshop owner. It brings out the profoundness of class and political cleavages and the power of the Church in Malta.

KININMONTH, CHRISTOPHER, 1957, *The Brass Dolphins: A Description of the Maltese Archipelago.* London: Secker and Warburg. Out of print.

An uneven, highly personal account of the author's three years in town and village in Malta. At times waspish, often perceptive, always informative; it is never dull.

LUKE, SIR HARRY, 1960, *Malta: An Account and an Appreciation,* 2d. ed. London: Harrap.

A collection of entertaining and informative essays on topics, mostly historical, which interested the author, a former lieutenant-governor of the islands.

PRICE, CHARLES A., 1954, *Malta and the Maltese: A Study in Nineteenth Century Migration.* Melbourne: Georgian House.

A scholarly treatise containing an admirable reconstruction of economic and social conditions in Malta a century ago, plus an excellent bibliography.

1979 Addendum

ACEVES, JOSEFH B., 1971, *Social Change in a Spanish Village*. Cambridge, Mass.: Schenkman Publishing Company.

————, and DOUGLASS, WILLIAM A., eds., 1976, *The Changing Faces of Rural Spain*. New York: Schenkman Publishing Company.

ALLUM, P. A., 1973, *Politics and Society in Post-War Naples*. Cambridge, Eng.: Cambridge University Press.

BAILEY, F. G., ed., 1971, *Gifts and Poison: The Politics of Reputation*. Oxford: Basil Blackwell.

————, 1973, *Debate and Compromise: The Politics of Innovation*. Oxford: Basil Blackwell.

BARRETT, RICHARD A., 1974, *Benbarre: The Modernization of a Spanish Village*. New York: Holt, Rinehart and Winston.

BLACK-MICHAUD, JACOB, 1975, *Cohesive Force: Feud in the Mediterranean and the Middle East*. Oxford: Basil Blackwell.

BLOK, ANTON, 1974, *The Fafia of a Sicilian Village, 1860–1960: A Study of Violent Peasant Entrepreneurs*. Oxford: Basil Blackwell.

BOISSEVAIN, JEREMY, and FRIEDL, JOHN, eds., 1975, *Beyond the Community: Social Process in Europe*. The Hague: Department of Education and Science for the Department of European and Mediterranean Studies, University of Amsterdam.

BRANDES, STANLEY H., 1975, *Migration, Kinship and Community: Tradition and Transition in a Spanish Village*. New York: Academic Press.

BROGGER, JAN, 1971, *Montevarese: A Study of Peasant Society and Culture in Southern Italy*. Bergen, Nor.: Universitetsforlaget.

CHAPMAN, CHARLOTTE GOWER, 1971, *Milocca: A Sicilian Village*. London: George Allen & Unwin.

CHRISTIAN, WILLIAM A., Jr., 1972, *Person and God in a Spanish Valley*. New York: Seminar Press.

COLE, JOHN W., and WOLF, ERIC R., 1974, *The Hidden Frontier: Ecology and Ethnicity in an Alpine Valley*. New York: Academic Press.

CUTILEIRO, JOSÉ, 1971, *A Portuguese Rural Society*. Oxford: Clarendon Press.

DAVIS, J., 1973, *Land and Family in Pisticci*. London: The Athlone Press.

————, 1977, *People of the Mediterranean: An Essay in Comparative Social Anthropology*. London: Routledge & Kegan Paul.

DOUGLASS, WILLIAM A., 1969, *Death in Murelaga: Funerary Ritual in a Spanish Basque Village*. Seattle: University of Washington Press.

————, 1975, *Echalar and Murelaga: Opportunity and Rural Exodus in Two Spanish Basque Villages*. New York: St. Martin.

DU BOULAY, JULIET, 1974, *Portrait of a Greek Mountain Village*. Oxford: Clarendon Press.

FRASER, RONALD, 1973, *Tajos: The Story of a Village on the Costa del Sol*. New York: Pantheon Books.

FREEMAN, SUSAN TAX, 1970, *Neighbors: The Social Contract in a Castilian Hamlet*. Chicago: The University of Chicago Press.

GELLNER, ERNEST, and WATERBURY, JOHN, 1977, *Patrons and Clients in Mediterranean Societies*. London: Duckworth, in association with the Center for Mediterranean Studies of the American Universities Field Staff.

GREENWOOD, DAVYDD J., 1978, *Unrewarding Wealth: The Commercialization and Collapse of Agriculture in a Spanish Basque Town*. Cambridge, Eng.: Cambridge University Press.

GROSS, FELIKS, 1973, *Il Paese: Values and Social Change in an Italian Village*. New York: New York University Press.

HALPERN, JOEL M., and HALPERN, BARBARA KEREWSKY, 1972, *A Serbian Village in Historical Perspective*. New York: Holt, Rinehart and Winston.

HAMMEL, EUGENE A., 1968, *Alternative Social Structure and Ritual Relations in the Balkans.* Englewood Cliffs, N.J.: Prentice-Hall.

HANSEN, EDWARD C., 1977, *Rural Catalonia Under the Franco Regime: The Fate of Regional Culture Since the Spanish Civil War.* Cambridge, Eng.: Cambridge University Press.

LOIZOS, PETER, 1975, *The Greek Gift: Politics in a Cypriot Village.* Oxford: Basil Blackwell.

LOPREATO, JOSEPH, 1967, *Peasants No More: Social Class and Social Change in an Underdeveloped Society.* San Francisco: Chandler Publishing Company.

MALEFAKIS, EDWARD E., 1970, *Agrarian Reform and Peasant Revolution in Spain: Origins of the Civil War.* New Haven, Conn.: Yale University Press.

MARASPINI, A. L., 1968, *The Study of an Italian Village.* Paris: Mouton & Co., in collaboration with the École Pratique des Hautes Études, Sorbonne VIe Section, Sciences Economiques et Sociales.

MARTINEZ-ALIER, JUAN, 1971, *Labourers and Landowners in Southern Spain.* London: George Allen & Unwin.

MENDRAS, HENRI, 1970, *The Vanishing Peasant: Innovation and Change in French Agriculture.* Cambridge, Mass.: The M.I.T. Press.